Online Law Practice Strategies:

How to Turn Clicks into Clients

2015 Edition

By Jabez LeBret and Mark Homer

Online Law Practice Strategies: How to Turn Clicks into Clients, 2015 Edition
By Jabez LeBret and Mark Homer

Legal Technology Press
1775 Mentor Avenue, Suite 302
Cincinnati, OH 45212 U.S.A.
expert@legaltechpress.com
Phone: 513-444-2016

Copyright © 2015 by Legal Technology Press
ISBN: 978-0-9826403-8-8
Library of Congress Control Number: 2015939074
Published in the United States of America

A SPECIAL THANK YOU:

Mark and I wanted to take a moment to say thank you to several of the people that really helped make this project a success.

To Haley Moore from GNGF: Thank you for working with us so patiently to get this revision completed. Your eye for design, project management abilities, and communication on this project made it what it is today.

To Jess Schaffner from GNGF: You are the best editor ever! Thank you for hustling to get this turned around and adding intelligent comments that pushed us to make a better book. Your eye and perspective both had a huge impact on this project.

To Chris C. and Chris H. from GNGF: Thank you for poring through all the great examples we had to identify the best images, charts, and graphics to support the concepts discussed in this book.

To our entire team: Thank you for putting up with us and keeping the company running smoothly, again, while we were working hard to create this book. This goes for our families as well; thanks for your patience—again—specifically to Jack and Ryan. Sorry your dad missed a few dinners at home while he was working late on the book.

A special thank you to all the bar associations that invited us to speak this past year. Because of those presentations, we were able to add fun lawyer stories of both successes and some misses.

Finally, thank you to Avvo, Clio, and Fujitsu for contributing to this book. Your additional input and services are of great value to the legal market. We are excited to continue to have your support and look forward to an amazing year.

TABLE OF CONTENTS

INTRODUCTION

Marketing and the Law Firm in the Internet Age

More has changed in the last 18 months with law firm marketing than in the past five years. This book is filled with the most up-to-date techniques to help any size law firm to establish an online presence.

Today, everyone—from the young to the not-so-young—uses the Internet to find information. Historically, a law firm did not advertise or market its services; in today's world, however, there is little to no future for a law firm without a solid online presence. Not too long ago, a law firm was able to see steady growth with a strong reputation and a healthy referral network. Now, with pricing pressure and a lack of loyalty, law firm clients and prospects are turning to the Internet for both legal information and new service providers. With technology, there is more than one door of access to a law office, and most people are arriving at law firm's offices via the Internet—even if they are arriving on the recommendation of a friend or colleague.

Suddenly, the first impression many people receive of your firm is *not* from walking through the front door but rather from your website and, more importantly, your overall web presence.

It was in 1993 when this crazy little thing called the World Wide Web browser was invented, marking the creation of a whole host of new doors to a law firm's office.

Did you know that the first graphical World Wide Web browser for Microsoft Windows was actually developed for the legal community? Tom Bruce, a system administrator-turned-programmer at the Legal Information Institute at Cornell, decided that the web was just what the Institute needed to distribute information to the legal community. He started work on "Cello," a native Windows-based browser, in June of 1993.

Just about 20 years later, the Internet has introduced opportunities to advertise your firm both through doors that you can control—such as your website, online videos, blogs, and more—and doors that you can only influence—like Google search returns, online directory listings, social media, and online review sites.

The Internet should seem like a natural step in the evolution of legal services. Search engines are the place people go when they have questions about a myriad of things ranging from how to fix things all the way to complex legal issues. Even online reviews and recommendations from "friends" on social media have become a new trusted word of mouth.

Similarly, we have found that more and more people are turning to the Internet to verify information they find elsewhere. For example, one of your friends or colleagues may recommend you to someone with a legal problem while at a networking event or social engagement. Your friend or colleague likely won't have your business card on hand. So where will this new prospect go to find your phone number? Google, of course. The prospect may not even wait to get home to look you up; instead, he or she will likely search for you on his or her mobile device right then and there. Depending on what your online presence looks like, he or she will determine whether or not you get a phone call.

Does your online presence reflect your firm's offline reputation?

Consider the following:

- When potential clients search for your name on Google, what comes up on the first page of search results?

- When they go to your website, does it look as professional as your office?

- When they click on Yelp, Avvo, or Google+ to see your reviews, what have others said about you?

- Can they watch a video that talks about who you are and how you help people with problems similar to theirs?

- If they search for you on Facebook, does your Facebook page show that you are active in the community?

Even if you do everything else really well, you may lose a potential client because of one search on Google. Frustrating, yes. But this is the reality.

This book will explore recent changes in law firm marketing and will provide practical instructions on establishing your law firm online in a way that maximizes this new reality.

Today, it is understood as fact that the Internet changes at a rapid pace. Because of this, we have challenged ourselves to update this book frequently (every 12 to 16 months so far). So, welcome to version 4.0 of this book, which contains the latest and greatest information on properly positioning your firm online. This revision is important because it addresses several major shifts in the world of online marketing, particularly for law firms. In the span of a year, Google has made more significant algorithm updates, mobile smartphones have crossed the chasm and cannot be ignored, and social media has grown and continued to influence behavior—among other important trends.

This book has the best of both worlds: the stable, tried-and-true principles of having a successful practice online and the impact of the latest updates and changes of this past year. We even included some advanced techniques GNGF is using with our own clients to get results.

Grab a pen, and start taking notes. (This book should look like you have rewritten it by the time you are finished, with notes added in the margins and corners folded.)

Of course, there will always be aspects of online marketing that change occasionally. To stay on top of any important changes, we recommend that you subscribe to our eNewsletter and follow our blog at https://gngf.com/blog/.

The information in this book and on our blog works, but—like everything you learned in law school—it only works when implemented. The difference between *average* practices and *great* practices comes down to implementation. One law firm differs from another often only in its willingness to implement the things that can be learned about reaching your prospects. This means that simply *knowing* all of this information won't help you achieve better results in your practice. When you *implement* these techniques and information, it will allow you to help more people, create a more stable firm, and gain some bragging rights at the next conference you attend.

Use this book, and send us your success story.

One of the most common questions that we get from lawyers who have read our book is, "How am I supposed to get all of this done?" In full disclosure, this book is part of our learning division, but we are also a marketing agency for law firms. We want you to learn first. We are obviously going to tell you about ourselves, but we will save that information for the end. The very last section is all about us, including our eLearning platform, IT services, consulting, and marketing services. Until then, we will simply share as much as we can on the what, why, and how of proven online law practice strategies.

Let's get started.

SECTION 1:
MARKETING ONLINE 2015

Your law firm brand is likely being misrepresented online because you are ignoring your law firm's web presence outside of your website. We see this everyday; law firms create a website and stop there, without ever searching for other places their firm may be represented online.

Google your firm name, partners, associates, and staff. You will likely find information online that you did not create—and lots of it. There are directory listings, scrapers, and other online sources that grab information from around the web and post this information to their websites. Some of this information is correct, but oftentimes it is either incomplete or flat out wrong.

Having an online presence is more than just creating a website. When people look for legal assistance, there are numerous ways they can find your law firm: they can search online, go to an app on their mobile phone, or interact with friends on social media. Many of these actions will give them enough information to decide whether or not they will contact your firm—all without ever having visited your website. Of course, a website is the foundation of your online presence; however, it is crucial that you understand that a website is *only one piece* of your overall web presence. In this section, we will discuss all the things that you need to think about—and implement—in order to maximize the impact of your law firm's web presence.

U.S. INTERNET USERS SPEND 1 OUT OF EVERY 8 MINUTES ONLINE USING FACEBOOK

88% OF CONSUMERS READ ONLINE REVIEWS FOR LOCAL BUSINESSES

97% OF CONSUMERS
RESEARCH THEIR PURCHASES AND LOCAL SERVICES ONLINE BEFORE THEY FULFILL THEM AT A LOCAL BUSINESS

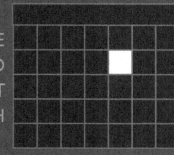

GOOGLE
HAS 85% OF ALL SEARCH TRAFFIC

39% OF CONSUMERS USE THE INTERNET TO FIND A LOCAL BUSINESS AT LEAST ONCE A MONTH

92% OF CONSUMERS USED THE INTERNET TO FIND A LOCAL BUSINESS IN THE LAST 12 MONTHS

MARKETING STRATEGY

DEMOGRAPHICS
OF YOUR BEST CLIENTS

UNIQUE
SELLING
PROPOSITION

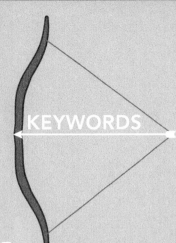

KEYWORDS

A WEBSITE WON'T DO ANYTHING FOR YOUR BUSINESS IF NO ONE FINDS IT

WHY REVIEWS MATTER

88%

OF CONSUMERS TRUST ONLINE REVIEWS AS **MUCH AS** **PERSONAL** RECOMMENDATIONS

72% SAY POSITIVE REVIEWS MAKE THEM TRUST A BUSINESS MORE

67% OF CONSUMERS READ 6 REVIEWS OR LESS TO MAKE UP THEIR MIND

Chapter 1:

The world has changed. Since the advent of the Internet and the adoption of social networks, there has been a fundamental shift in how and when people choose to find information about legal issues. To help identify where you should be spending your efforts online, it is vital to step back and think about your potential clients' behavior. The most important question to ask yourself is this: where and how are my potential clients finding answers to their legal problems?

Friends and Colleagues Referring Your Firm

Getting referrals is still the most powerful technique for building a successful law firm. But why are we talking about referrals in an online marketing book?

Five to ten years ago, a prospective client who was referred to your firm would look up your phone number in the phonebook and call you. This phone call or office visit was your chance to leave a good first impression. Now, however, referrals are checking you out without you even knowing it. They are not calling or dropping by the office; instead, they are looking you up online.

Here is how referrals work in 2015:

Larry owns a company that earns $8 million per year in gross revenue. He and his business partners are splitting up the organization over a dispute about the future of the company.

While at a barbeque, Larry asks his friend Robert if he knows any good business attorneys that may be able to help with his situation. Robert tells Larry about a situation he faced a couple of years ago and how his attorney, Sarah, really helped out.

Larry grabs his phone out of his pocket and opens up a search browser, typing Sarah's full name into the mobile device. He then clicks on the first link that appears.

Armed with just a name, today's consumer will search for you or your firm on Google or Bing; check review sites like Yelp, Google+, or Avvo; and visit your website—generally well before they even think about calling you. If they don't like what they see during their searches, they may never call you. Maybe you don't have any reviews, and the firm just above or below you in search results has a lot of positive reviews. Or, maybe your site looks like a basic template that could have been designed in 10 minutes using tools from GoDaddy or Wix. At the end of the day, even though you have done a great job for your clients and built a strong referral network, you are likely losing referrals due to a poor online presence.

You are losing referral business you didn't even know you had because your web presence is missing key pieces or is out of date when people look for you online.

Paying attention to the details of your web presence helps you mitigate possible losses to your referral business. This is not to imply that you need to spend hundreds of hours or $200,000 on your web presence. Rather, you need to dominate the first page of Google search results, have a mobile-ready presence, and provide social proof that demonstrates you are a trusted source for legal counsel. Try having someone other than yourself look you up on a mobile device or laptop and see what the results show.

It is worth noting that younger generations (Gen X and Millennials) who grew up with computer technology are now between the ages of 22 and 55. These generations are your current and future clients. They, more than other generations, are relying on technology, the Internet, and social signals to make important decisions. It does not matter if you agree with this practice; it is reality. Just ask a doctor how often someone comes into their office having already researched their condition on WebMD. It has probably happened to you in your law practice. Your prospect or client approaches you with a legal problem that they have already researched. Your prospects have a new approach to finding solutions to their legal problems, regardless of being referred to someone: it's called "search."

Enter the Search Engines

For those of us who remember a time before the Internet, it is amazing to think that people now turn to the web for information regarding potentially sensitive and often complex legal issues. Little by little, search engines—and other companies like Amazon and Facebook—have trained us to use the Internet to get answers to any problem. Need a book on your doorstep tomorrow? Use the Internet. Need directions to that new restaurant downtown? Use the Internet. Missed the big game and want to know the score? You guessed it: use the Internet. Now, it provides answers to legal problems as well.

Using the Internet to research a legal issue has an advantage over other methods of inquiry: privacy. Legal issues are very different from many other challenges that consumers face. For problems with their plumbing or car, it is extremely common to consult a friend or colleague. However, many legal matters—like business litigation, bankruptcy, criminal charges, or divorce—are personal problems that people want to keep to themselves. What better way to keep potentially embarrassing issues private than to use a machine to search for answers? We also have to consider that the Internet is proving to be successful in helping people address their questions and issues. Today, 88 percent of consumers trust online reviews as much as personal recommendations, which is an increase of 10 percent from last year alone. Obviously, consumers feel that online research is benefiting them.

When researching online, the first place that many people go is a search engine. Popular search engines include Google, Yahoo!, and Bing. Here, they type in their issue or question. The reality is that users are still going to Google as their primary source. Across all our clients—it is worth stressing here that we only work with law firms—traffic from Google accounts for over 78 percent of all search engine traffic. We are not alone. We've spoken with companies like Attorney Sync, Nifty Law, and others who are all seeing similar data. That does not mean you should ignore Bing and Yahoo!, but you should focus on Google before the others.

Search engines are unique in that they serve to help the user solve any problem or answer any question. This is in contrast to other websites that have specific purposes: ESPN gives you a recap of the game, Amazon sells you a product, Facebook facilitates interactions with your friends and family, and so on. Search engines are highly effective at helping people solve a problem—any problem—which is why they are so popular. It is crucial that businesses and professionals use them to their advantage.

When people need help solving a legal problem, they often begin by doing a general search about the issue or question they have. They may not even be sure that they need a lawyer at the beginning of their search; however, once they spend some time researching a complex legal problem, they will likely come to the obvious conclusion that they need an attorney's help.

A typical search engine results page (SERP)—what shows up when you type something into Google—will include a variety of things that can help answer the question posed by the searcher. There may be a recent news article, links to videos, links to websites that deal with that issue, images, paid advertisements, or links to a few long articles or blog posts. See *Figure 1*.

The marketing effort you spend to increase your visibility in search engine results is different than the effort put into other forms of marketing, such as interrupt marketing. For instance, your TV program is cut off for a " commercial break," the magazine article you are reading is interspersed with print ads, or your Facebook feed is filled with display ads that are vying for your attention. These are all examples of interrupt marketing that you experience all the time and may not even realize it.

It makes sense that interrupt advertising is going to be less effective than search visibility. With search, the user is declaring that he or she has a specific problem at that moment and is seeking a solution. With interrupt marketing, you are hoping to catch that reader at the right time, or you are simply looking to build TOMA (top-of-mind awareness). There is importance to TOMA, but that is a passive play with slower results. For larger firms, this should remain part of your overall strategy, but your investment should be shifting from traditional advertising to a more relevant and effective medium.

Being the firm that comes up in search engine results with the answer to someone's question is extremely powerful. To the searcher, Google and other search engines are essentially putting their stamp of approval on your firm's content if you show up on the coveted first page of results.

Figure 1: Standard Google search

We do not consider the yellow pages to be an interrupt ad. In fact, it was one of the original local business "search engines" for consumers. In previous versions of this book, we spent time discussing statistics about the yellow pages, including its clear decline in use and effectiveness. But now, it is becoming so irrelevant that we will assume everyone knows that the paper version of the yellow pages is very near death. The following story should illustrate this fact:

> **At a cookout, I was talking to a friend about how much is still spent in the paper yellow pages industry. Amusingly, his 14-year-old son piped in and asked with total sincerity, "What are the yellow pages?"**

Millennials have always had computers and cellphones around, and they use the Internet for everything. We should constantly remind ourselves that those at the front end of the Millennial demographic have already entered their thirties. This demographic comprises more than 80 million people in the U.S. If you believe that you still need to have a full-page spread in the yellow pages to target potential senior clients, you should rethink that investment. On Twitter, the 55–64 age bracket has been the fastest growing demographic since 2012. The fastest growing demographic on Facebook and Google+ is the 45–54 age bracket (from a 2013 GlobalWebIndex study).

Of those who are 65 years of age and older, some still use the yellow pages. If this demographic represents a significant portion of your clients, by all means, print an ad in the yellow pages. But reduce the size of the ad the next time your contract comes up; that will free funds in your marketing budget to invest in future advertising endeavors. Also, think about who is doing the research on the legal issue. Mom and dad who are in their eighties? The kids who are in their fifties? Or even the grandchildren who are in their twenties? This makes a difference when it comes to choosing your marketing strategy.

You may have noticed that we will be focusing on Google for the majority of this book. This is because of its dominance over Internet search. Our data also shows that the strategies that work for Google will carry over nicely to other search engines. Though you've probably seen news reports saying that, on average, people spend more time every day viewing Facebook and other social media sites, it is essential to understand that Google's importance has not diminished at all. This is because, for now, Google search and Facebook serve very different functions.

Typically, a user visits a website like Facebook to review information that has been posted by friends and family members. You may check Twitter for news or industry information and Google+ or LinkedIn for work-related posts. When you visit Google, however, your only goal is to search for something and find a website offering information on the subject for which you searched.

The average user, searching for a criminal defense attorney or a car accident lawyer, is getting search returns on Google within milliseconds. Immediately, that user looks at the local returns (A, B, C, D, and so on) or the overall SERP page for topics relating to their issue. Then, the user will typically click on the link to the law firm that is found on Page 1 via organic search, or the user will click on the A, B, or C slot of local results. This entire process might take 5 to 15 seconds, maximum. If the user does not like the website or reviews seen on the first click, he or she will navigate back to the search results and most likely click the next search return. In total, he or she is probably spending less than 25 seconds per search.

See *Figure 2* & *Figure 3*.

This is why being ranked on Page 1 is so important and why having a strategy that keeps the prospect on your website is crucial. (We will discuss website design later.) The average user may click on the search returns at the bottom of the organic listings, but almost never navigates to the second page of search results. According to a study done in June 2013 by Chitika, the first page of Google search results garnered 92 percent of traffic. On that first page, the firms listed will receive almost all the traffic.

Google knows that people come to its search engine to get answers to their questions. If they don't find the answer quickly, they will stop coming to Google and go somewhere else. Interestingly enough, 95 percent of Google's yearly $50 billion revenue comes from advertising. (Sometimes, when people search on Google, they see a small text ad that seems relevant for their search, and they click on it. The advertiser pays Google when that ad is clicked. This is the pay-per-click, or PPC, model. We will discuss this later in the book.) If people stop coming to Google to search, the company loses its revenue source. This is why Google is highly motivated to provide the best search results possible and avoid allowing spammy websites to rank.

Think back to just five years ago, when your searches would occasionally return a website that was junk. Maybe the page was filled with links to things that were not relevant, or maybe the website made you do a secondary search to find an answer. These junk websites often came up in search returns as a result of someone gaming the system. Companies and people who try to game the system perform spam or "black hat" SEO. To combat this, Google makes significant updates throughout the year. The company works to make searching

Figure 2: Google search results with local pack

Figure 3: Google search results without local pack

a better experience for the user—faster and more relevant. In the past several years, Google has made some of the most comprehensive anti-spam and search engine updates to date. We consider these updates a great thing for searchers and for law firms. Google is trying to reward real businesses that do things the right way. This is beneficial for the people doing the searching, who get the answers they need; for the ethical law firm, who gets to help more people; and for Google, which keeps its ad revenue.

The following section describes a few of the major changes that Google has made over the past three years. Understanding these changes will help you make the appropriate strategy adjustments to maintain or gain a high ranking. Ignoring these changes will ensure that your website falls further in the rankings over the next 12 months. Included is the biggest update Google has made to its search algorithm—ever.

Major Updates from Google

The fact is that Google is constantly changing its algorithms to increase its effectiveness. This means that, several times each day, Google makes slight adjustments to its algorithm to return the best possible results for a search. In fact, we see the company testing algorithm changes all the time. Google has admitted to performing thirteen thousand algorithm tests in just one year. Occasionally, we will search in one market or area of the country, and our results will look completely different from searches in another part of the country. Most of the time, that is the result of Google testing something new.

From time to time, Google makes a major update. This does not happen very often, although it has dramatically increased in frequency within the past two years. What constitutes a major update? In the past, Google would announce one of these updates, explain its major goals, and give it a name. Now, with increased frequency, Google is simply rolling out updates and talking about them after the fact.

Immediately following a major update, you will typically see a shift in the search rankings of a large number of websites. These are positive changes for you as an attorney. Why? Because each change makes it more difficult for people to cheat the system and get ranked when they have not done the work or when they have lied about their actual location.

While there is a lot of detail we could go into regarding these updates, here is what you need to know as a law firm or internal marketing department:

(Algorithm updates listed in order of oldest to most recent to show the progression of change.)

Panda

The Panda update, initially rolled out in February 2011, had a massive impact on overall search returns, affecting 12 percent of searches in just its first two months. This update affected directory services and content farms that increased their rankings by aggregating content from other webpages and/or producing subpar content that was keyword-heavy. These types of websites were getting ranked because they had tons of content—but they were copying and pasting articles or writing content of no value to the reader. The websites would make money from ads or from selling lead generation numbers to businesses. If, in the past 10 years, you were ever approached by someone claiming to have the number one website for "best [insert practice area] attorney in [insert city]" while telling you that you could lease the site to get leads, there's a good chance their website was a spammy content farm. These websites no longer rank; only websites with unique, frequently updated, quality content are ranking highly. With the Panda update, Google was looking to prevent one company from reaping the benefits of everyone else's hard work and to prevent companies from writing useless content just to get ranked.

Panda 4.1 was rolled out sometime in early September 2014. This rollout affected 3–5 percent of total search. This is important to note: Google appears to still be regularly updating the Panda algorithm.

What you need to know about the Panda update and your firm's web presence is simple: Google requires websites to produce useful, relevant, high-quality content.

Query Encryption

In October 2011, Google announced that it would be encrypting search queries for privacy reasons. Unfortunately, this disrupted organic keyword referral data, returning "(not provided)" for some organic traffic. The number of affected returns increased in the weeks following the launch. Initially estimated to make up only 15 to 20 percent of searches, this secure Google search happened when the searcher was logged into Google property or used a browser that took advantage of the Google secure search. As Gmail, Google Drive, Google+, and YouTube required users to be logged in, the amount of secure searches increased to more than 50 percent. By the end of 2013, some sites were reporting that secure search was affecting at least 85 percent of their traffic. Recently, Google indicated that it expects nearly 100 percent of Google searches to be secure. What this means for you is that keyword data—or what people were searching for when they found your website—is practically gone.

This is a big piece of data that firms have lost under the guise of "protecting the searcher." While we believe that Google had some good intentions, it should be noted that if a business pays Google via AdWords, then it does get keyword data, regardless of whether the search was secure or not.

See *Figure 4.*

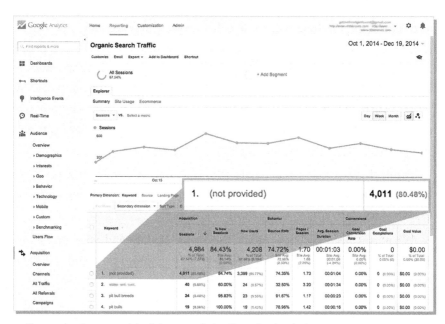

Figure 4: (not provided) keywords in Google Analytics

Freshness

At the end of 2011, Google announced that it was making a change that impacted 35 percent of search queries. That is quite a large impact for an algorithm update. (Panda shook the industry and only affected 12 percent of queries.) The Freshness update, as it is was named, prioritized recent, relevant content. This update often goes unmentioned, but it was a big push toward fresh content. With the Panda and Freshness updates, Google has emphasized content that is both original and timely.

Penguin

In April 2012, we saw the next big Google algorithm update: Penguin. This update was said to initially affect only 3–4 percent of websites. The Penguin update was entirely focused on combating what Google called "black hat webspam" on its official search blog. Through this update, Google really began to crack down on the practice of duplicating content. Google believes that "white hat" SEO (what we recommend) improves the usability of a website and provides value to both users and the search engine. The company wanted to attack webspam without attacking white hat SEO. The Penguin update focused on devaluing black hat SEO tactics (like keyword stuffing and link schemes). Link building the easy way (buying links from black hat SEOs) became ineffective and resulted in immediate penalization of your site. Also, sites that engaged in stuffing keywords related to their practice areas and cities were affected.

Figure 5 & *Figure* 6 provide a definition and a common example of keyword stuffing.[1]

Something very important to understand is that the Penguin update had massive implications for local search returns. Pay attention, because this is a big deal.

We mentioned that Google changed its search algorithm through the Panda update to reduce poor quality and duplicate content. And because of the Penguin update, this practice is now more dangerous than ever. If two websites have the same content, Google will only give credit to one of the websites.

For example, let's say that you have an "Our Services" page on your website. On this page, you copied and pasted the exact content from another one of your

---

[1]   https://support.google.com/webmasters/answer/66358

Figure 5: Keyword stuffing definition by Google

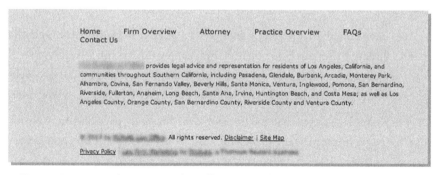

Figure 6: Image 4b - Keyword Stuffing Example.jpg

firm's websites—or worse, from another law firm's page. Google will only give one firm credit for that content, and often, the credit goes to the person that posted first. (In some cases, the largest website will get the credit.) Therefore, posting duplicate content is a waste of your time that does not produce any results or give you any credit for your ranking. This is time that you could have spent doing something that would add value to your web presence. In the SEO industry, it is suspected that Google will eventually penalize websites for duplicate content, but that theory has not been proven true—yet.

Another important piece to the Penguin update concerns linking strategies. Your linking strategy encompasses both inbound links (links to your website from other websites) and internal cross-linking (links from one page on your website to another page on your website). The Penguin update provides a set of best practices regarding how, when, and how often you should link within your own website as well as how you should be obtaining inbound links.

First, let's talk about backlinking (also known as inbound linking). In short, a backlink is any link to your website from another website. This could be a link to your website from the local chamber of commerce, a bar association, another blogger, etc. Backlinks are crucial to your SEO plan and are one of the backbones of any good online strategy. In fact, measuring backlinks was the initial way that Google differentiated its algorithm-based search engine when it was created. It is still probably one of the most significant factors that Google uses to determine rank. However, companies have found ways to game the system and get backlinks through automated processes, large networks in which one company controls all the websites, and cheap human capital.

To prevent companies from cheating the system, Google now grades the quality of the links that point back to your website and attributes their value toward your website's value. If all your backlinks are from websites that Google deems worthless, your website will drop in the rankings.

Now more than ever, worthless backlinks are extremely damaging to your website's ranking. They will kill your web presence, so avoid them at all costs. We will cover how to properly build backlinks to your website later in the book.

Internal linking is when you link from one part of your website to another. A common example of internal linking is your website navigation. You may have noticed that a lot of websites will include the very same links used in the navigation in the footer. Adding a link to most of your internal pages in the footer section of your website used to be a great way to boost your internal links—but not anymore. Google has said that your website navigation should be in one place, easy to use, and preferably located at the top of the page. Now, why would Google care if your navigation to the pages on your website is at the top of the page?

When you are ranked highly on the first page of Google's search returns, Google is, in a sense, endorsing your website as the best option for that search term. If Google returns and endorses websites that are difficult to navigate, the user might start using a different search engine, like Bing. That is why Google wants your website to be easy to use and navigate. This increases the amount of time people spend on your website and the number of pages they visit, which are things that Google tracks. When a person spends quite a bit of time on the pages of a website, this signals to Google that it is doing its job: providing the best possible answer to that person's search query. It is well-known in the website development community that navigation at or near the top of the website creates an optimal user experience. Because of the Penguin update, navigation links in the footer of your website no longer add value.

The Penguin update also began devaluing websites that have improper or poorly designed internal links from one page to the next. There are some online marketing firms that will cram as many internal links as possible on one page. But Google has said it would prefer, just as with the links in the footer of the page, that most of the internal linking be done within the navigation. That doesn't mean that you can't include links in the content of your page—just don't go overboard. And when you do include links in the copy of your website, the link names should be unique and relevant: all of your links should not be titled "Adoption Attorney Sacramento, CA," for example. For example, if you are writing about an attorney's specific practice area on his or her profile page, it is perfectly acceptable to title your link "Adoption Attorney Sacramento, CA." However, if you are writing a blog post about adoption and want to link to your adoption practice area page, the link should match the content of that page:

> There is no fast track to adoption. Even though adoption in the state of California can take up to three years, it is possible to…

In the above examples, the links go to the same page, but the titles of the links change according to the context. It is not a requirement that the link title be conversational, but it is certainly an easy solution to this linking practice.

Similarly, Google prefers that the images on your website have unique names. In the past, too many websites were crammed with images that all contained the same keywords. It used to be common practice to title each image with basic keywords like "[Practice Area] Attorney [City], [State]." Now, you need to make sure that each image has a unique title that includes your keywords and a description relevant to the image itself. Also, if the image is one that you took and that you own, include your firm's name in the image title and description. This is more work but is well worth the value added.

Venice

Announced in February 2012, this update flew under the radar, most likely due to the hysteria over Google's many adjustments to the Panda updates. This update was specific to local search.

Because of the Venice update, when you search using terms like "divorce attorney" without including a city location, Google gives you local returns within the organic returns. Because of the Pigeon update, which we will cover later, it is difficult to tell the exact effects of the Venice update.

This update made several things very clear to website developers with regards to how search engines want to see your address and location on your website:

1) You should include rich snippets on your website. "Rich snippets" is a fancy term for adding your address in the hCard microformat or schema format of the actual coding of your website. (This is something you should ask your website developer to handle.) These formats make it easier for Google to figure out where your firm is and what it does. In the last version of our book, we didn't take a side on whether to use hCard or schema. Now, we typically recommend that you use the schema format.

2) Be sure to embed a Google map of your office. Another good idea is to give written directions to your location on your contact page. This helps Google see a broader picture of your physical location. Give driving directions from two points in town to your office. If you have more than one office, give driving directions to each on different pages.

Overuse of your location in your website copy can be damaging to your overall ranking. Google has not said how much is too much; however, a good rule of thumb is to always make sure that the use of your location in your copy is as conversational and natural as possible.

Knowledge Graph

In May 2012, Google made a major update to further its goal of providing the best answer to a searcher's question as quickly as possible. If Google thinks it has information that can supplement search results about a certain person, business, or thing, it now includes that information in what is known as a "Knowledge Graph" in the search results.

This Knowledge Graph is somewhat troubling to websites. Today, a user doesn't even have to visit a website listed in the search results to see the score of the big game from last night, the weather, movie times, or the phone number, reviews, or operating hours of a local law firm. In some instances, a Knowledge Graph may even give information about a specific legal issue. We have seen these graphs appear more and more. In the graphs, a searcher can see a critical amount of influential information about a law firm (its description, reviews, photos, etc.)—without even visiting the firm's website.

See *Figure 7*.

Note: it is no coincidence that much of the information found in the Knowledge Graph of a local law firm is the same information that you can define in the schema on your website.

In July 2013, the Knowledge Graph received a major update and now shows up in significantly more search queries. Our findings show that if you are doing everything right regarding your local web presence and website, then a Knowledge Graph will appear in a search for your firm name.

Penguin 2.1 Update

In October 2013, Penguin 2.1 was released. Initially, the impact was expected to be moderate, but we have heard from many law firms that have seen a meaningful drop in rankings. Those affected by the update had a history of questionable link building of which they were completely unaware, as such activity is often the behind-the-scenes work of an SEO company. Law firms with such issues can eventually restore their rankings by cleaning up these bad back links, but it is a slow and laborious process.

Hummingbird

In August 2013, Google announced the most comprehensive update to its search algorithm to date. In fact, the company indicated that Hummingbird is a completely new algorithm—not an update to an old version. To understand the scope of this change, think of the furnace in your house. For years, it may have had some issues. You've gone in and fixed a part here and there, tightened some things, and cleaned it a bit, but you are just maintaining the furnace that you have. This is what Google has been doing to its main search algorithms since 2001—just tweaking and fixing parts as they break.

Figure 7: Example of Knowledge Graph

nity. After an issue with Yelp not showing up correctly in the SERPs, Google released an update to fix some issues with local search. As a result, we saw weeks of online chaos and a seemingly steady stream of fixes and adjustments to the Pigeon update.

The initial rollout of this update caused many of the local 7-pack listings to disappear. Say, for example, that a user searched for a "contract negotiation lawyer" or "personal injury attorney." Instead of seeing a map on the right side with listings of local law firms, the user started seeing only paid advertisements and organic listings. At the same time the update seemed to vault directory listings like Avvo and Lawyers.com to the top of rankings on the first page of results. This was extremely odd because only a month prior, Lawyers.com was virtually non-existent on Page 1 of search results; then, out of nowhere, they suddenly landed back on Page 1. This also meant that Google was making it harder for local firms to appear on the first page of SERPs without paying for PPC ad space, causing many people to believe that Google was looking to boost its PPC revenue. This theory can neither be confirmed nor disputed.

About three weeks into the updated versions of the previous local search return, 7-pack began to reemerge as 1-pack, 3-pack, and rarely a full 7-pack. Was this Google's attempt to pull back the Pigeon rollout? Or was the search engine simply improving the update to the algorithm? It doesn't really matter. If anything, this was a good reminder that you cannot set a plan for SEO without expecting to change courses throughout the year. This also means you need to look into doing some PPC advertising on Google in 2015.

The good news is several legal marketing agencies shared insights to their client traffic before and after Pigeon. The end results, excluding the data for the two chaotic weeks immediately following the most recent Pigeon update, showed that clients saw no noticeable change in traffic volumes. There was movement in some clients' traffic, both positive and negative, but in the end there was no evidence of consistent change. What will need to be determined is the shift in traffic over a six-month period. Because this book is printed, we will not be able to update the content here with that data. GNGF is running a long test to gain more insights. This information will be published on our blog when it becomes available, so please check our blog for an update on the Pigeon rollout. Another great resource for information about this update is Gyi Tsakalakis' blog, found at http://gyitsakalakis.com/.

Penguin 3.0

P3 aka Penguin 3.0 is the latest of the Penguin updates, rolled out in October 2014. This appears to be an add-on to the existing update and will be affecting more of the same types of activities. Interestingly, Google provided a disavow tool in the fall of 2013, which gives a webmaster the ability to cut the connection to a backlink he or she no longer wishes to have linking back to his or her website. This tool allowed webmasters to send Google a list of links that they believed were spammy in nature. In a way, it gives you the chance to say, "I'm sorry Google, I didn't mean to build that particular backlink; can you please remove my link from that spammy website?"

As a result, the online marketing community has been providing Google with a huge database of potentially spammy websites. Once P3 rolled out, it likely included many of the websites that were submitted within the disavow tool. This was an easy way for Google to crowdsource the quality of links.

WHAT DO ALL OF THESE UPDATES MEAN FOR YOU?

We know that this information may be exciting and important to us SEO geeks who spend all day thinking about and researching what Google and other search engines are doing. But, we understand that you are busy and may have just skimmed the previous section. Here is what you need to comprehend:

- Google truly wants to provide the best piece of information that it feels will answer the searcher's question.

- Google has been trying to keep people from gaming the system for years. In 2011, it started penalizing websites for spammy, black hat tactics.

- If you are paying for links, creating spammy, barely readable content, or stuffing your pages with too many keywords (in other words, creating websites for the benefit of search engines and not real people), then Google is going to go after your website.

- Google has removed an important data point for businesses: secured search is expected to apply to almost all searches in the very near future, meaning that you will no longer have access to keyword data. If you use AdWords, you will have access to some of that information—but not all.

- Hummingbird is the future of search. The new algorithm tries to derive meaning from a search that is not specified by the searchers, such as where they are located, what they do and share on social media, and what previous searches they have conducted.

- Local 7-pack listings may not last forever. Never put all your SEO eggs into one basket.

- Providing fresh, relevant content that is based on what you do and where you are located for your potential prospects is still important. How you provide that content, where you publish, how long, and how often will be discussed at length in this book.

That sums up the most important changes and updates that we feel relate specifically to attorneys and law firms.

However, that isn't everything you need to be thinking about.

Google has said many times, both verbally and in print, that it is striving to reward real, local businesses that have a quality service or product to offer to their communities. As a result, it is cracking down very harshly on anyone who tries to game the system with shady methods, such as buying links or creating fake listings. In the past, Google may have simply ignored these actions. While they didn't help, these actions may not have hurt your rankings. Now, however, both of these actions, among others, can result in penalization and a drop in the rankings—or Google may entirely delist you from its search index.

Though this may seem harsh or unreasonable, remember that Google's efforts to clean up its search algorithm only benefit you. You want the search engine to go after the black hat web spammers so that you, a real law firm that offers value and quality to consumers, can rise to the top, allowing people who are genuinely looking for your help and services to find you.

What About Pay Per Click or Other Paid Advertising?

From big firms to small firms, advertising online via paid ads can drive targeted clients to your website while providing you with valuable information. There are several forms of online advertising at your disposal.

This section is going to cover the techniques for establishing a paid campaign as well as various places you can allocate your budget. It is worth noting that you should consult a professional before hitting the go button. If you set up your campaigns incorrectly, you may be throwing money away—or worse, spending much more money than you expected. We are not trying to scare you but rather inform you that online paid advertising is not for rookies.

The various methods for paid advertising online break into two distinct categories: pay by click and pay by impression. These are referred to as "pay per click" (PPC) and "cost per impressions" (CPM). (Note that CPM is typically calculated by cost-per-thousand impressions.) Most platforms that allow paid advertising allow for both types of advertising; we will walk through each area by platform.

Google Paid Advertising

PPC on Google

As mentioned earlier, Google makes the majority of its money from PPC advertising. To put it bluntly, Google would not be able to continue to make billions and billions of dollars if PPC did not work for businesses. Depending on your current rankings, traffic, and volume of business, PPC may or may not be right for you. The benefit of PPC is that you get to control when searchers see information about your firm. It can also be the fastest way to drive new clients from the Internet when you begin building your long-term online presence. Of course, it is a very competitive and optimized marketplace. The keywords that tend to drive the most traffic—and lead to the best prospects—often have a fairly high cost. If you don't know what you are doing, you can easily spend far too much money in this area.

For most areas in the legal market, a law firm should expect to spend a minimum of $1,000 and up to $20K or $50K a month on PPC advertising. Sadly, we cannot narrow this range for you, but we *can* tell you about factors that influence the amount you should be paying.

However, a law firm can really screw up online paid advertising, so we want to first take a moment to walk you through a few hazards.

- **Exuberant agency fees:** Watch out for agencies that hide their fee structure or charge more than 30 percent of total ad spend. If you are budgeting less than $10,000 a month in ad spend, you should be paying between 15-20 percent toward the management fee. Demand transparency from your agency.

- **Not paying enough for your campaigns:** We hear lots of law firms complain that their Google PPC campaigns are not producing any results; then we find out they are only spending $1,000 a month with an agency. This is not much in the world of advertising. If you are not spending enough money to properly position your ads and garner enough clicks, you will not see positive results.

- **Laziness:** To properly run effective online advertising, you must really understand the behavior of your target client. If your practice area is DUI, focus ads on the times of day people are most likely to need your service, including all day Monday. If you are a contract attorney, focus on weekdays. Think about when, where, how, and what you are targeting.

- **Sending traffic to your homepage:** If you are paying for direct traffic through online ads, you *must* send this traffic to specific landing pages with proper tracking. How else are you going to know if your ads are performing well? Typically, we recommend these pages be set to "no-index." Check with your agency on these specifics.

- **Too few platforms:** Google PPC is not the only online paid advertising option. Research your other options and make a decision based on your target client, budget, and desired outcome.

The factors that drive the amount you need to spend include: competition, placement, your geographic location, amount of clicks, and quality score of your campaigns.

When there is a lot of competition for a keyword or phrase, the price goes up in a bidding war. This is why keywords like "mesothelioma" can cost upwards of $123 per click. That means for the top spot, for every time someone clicks on a law firm's ad for the search term "mesothelioma," that click costs a lot of money. For most areas of law, the cost is closer to $6 per click and up to $30 per click. Any agency that has experience with PPC on Google should be able to give you an approximate cost per click for your firm.

Display Ads and CPM on Google

Google provides you an opportunity to do something called "retargeting" with your paid ads. Though retargeting is not limited to CPM, this is a preferred method for using retargeting. When a visitor lands on your website, you are able to drop a "cookie" (small piece of code) on his or her web browser. This cookie gives you the opportunity to display ads to that user on other websites as they navigate around the Internet. You've likely experienced this without knowing what was happening. If you have ever visited a website and then noticed that the company's ads seemed to be following you around the Internet, you experienced retargeting in the works.

For an example, visit this page: http://gngf.com/bookretargeting

Now start navigating around the web. Over the next week, you will notice ads—designed specifically for that page on our GNGF website—following you around the web.

Retargeting is something that requires in-depth planning. Otherwise, you run the risk of annoying your target client or spending money displaying ads beyond their usefulness. If you are an estate planning attorney and someone visits your website page about "Establishing Trusts," then you should display ads for as long as you can. Each ad should directly target people looking to establish trusts because that is the page they visited on your website. The reason you do not need to worry about a time limit is simple; this type of client is typically not in a hurry to hire a lawyer. If you practice DUI defense, you may consider only running retargeting ads for 24 hours. The person who is arrested for a DUI will not likely be looking for an attorney three months after the offense. Remember, these are people that already visited your website.

But how often should you display your ad to a visitor? The frequency of retargeting ads is a common debate among online professionals. WordStream shared some fantastic data at Pubcon 2014 that basically put the argument to rest—users don't seem to care if you keep the ad going. What this means is that you do not need to throttle back the ad over time. As users navigate around the Internet, they will naturally begin seeing other ads and, over time, your ad will simply disappear into the background anyway.

Avvo Advertising

Avvo has been doing really, really, well online. This is why we recommend you advertise with Avvo. Promoted listings allow you the opportunity to get your personal Avvo profile in front of individuals looking for legal services. These prospects may come from Avvo's Legal Q&A Forum or directly from Google to Avvo. Either way, there are a few things worth pointing out about this platform.

The first thing we have noticed is that the quality of leads from Avvo paid advertising is higher than other platforms. Our clients across the board have seen better results with regards to quality. We have also noticed that Avvo's platform does not send the volume of leads a Google campaign can, so there is a near equalizer here. If you are only interested in volume, this may not be the best platform for you. For most firms, a combination of volume and quality is what matters—that makes Avvo a perfect opportunity.

You are also able to leverage the Avvo Ignite platform for a discount. This will help you track your leads. There is a whole chapter at the end of this book about the Ignite platform and tracking leads, so we will not go into great detail here.

Avvo has chosen to limit the total number of advertisers in any specific geographic territory. This means that you should expect the cost to advertise with Avvo to rise over time—no different than the bidding activity on Google. In the end, if the ROI makes sense, do it. For our clients, we have never recommended that someone stop advertising with Avvo after they began their campaigns, as the returns were quite obvious.

Social Media Advertising

All the major social networks, with the exceptions of Instagram and Pinterest, allow for some form of advertising. Even though you can purchase social media ads, we do not recommend advertising on most networks because there does not seem to be a high enough ROI to justify the hassle. Facebook is the best option for social paid advertising. In the social media section, under advanced tactics, there are full instructions for advertising on Facebook the right way.

Other Search Engines

We talk quite a lot about Google because it gets the lion's share of search traffic online. However, this doesn't mean that you should forget about other search engines, including Bing, Yahoo!, and even mobile search.

We will discuss mobile search later because it requires you to adhere to a very different set of rules than desktop search. When it comes to desktop search, you need to know one thing only: do exactly what we are about to tell you in the rest of the book, and your website will begin to rise in the Google rankings (and the rankings of every other search engine).

Social Media: The New Word of Mouth?

Another key area where people (your potential clients) go to find answers to their questions is social media. These networks barely existed 10 years ago but are now considered the new word of mouth marketing by many. We will spend an entire section of this book talking about social media, but we wanted to take a moment to explain its importance and growing relevance.

There are several very important reasons you must incorporate a social media strategy into your marketing efforts.

You simply can't ignore the sheer volume of people who are consistently active on various social media networks. For example, recent Facebook filings report that there are over one billion active users on Facebook. But here is the more impressive number: these active users spend an average of seven hours per month on the platform. That is almost 15 minutes a day, every day of the week.

Nearly half of these daily users are checking Facebook from mobile devices, not desktops. According to comScore, U.S. Internet users spend one out of every eight minutes online using Facebook. Users spend this time posting updates, interacting with photos, checking in to local businesses, commenting on what their friends post, reading what their friends recommend, and even interacting with companies that they care about or follow. Add Twitter, LinkedIn, Pinterest, and even Google+ to the mix and you have an incredibly large audience of people spending a lot of time discussing their problems and finding answers to their questions.

Search engines have taken notice of social media's prevalence. If links to websites were fuel for search algorithms in the past, then shares, mentions, and followers on social media could be the fuel of the future. Essentially, social media participation could become the new "links." The thoughts and activity of the people who are connected to your law firm could someday influence your own search results.

Both Google and Bing have said that they need (and want) to account for social signals in future search algorithms. In fact, Bing's Duane Forrester has indicated that Microsoft's search engine already incorporates social signals in its search algorithms. Google has been a bit more tight-lipped about this, but we believe that it is inevitable.

Online Reviews: Yes, We Really Trust Strangers

Like social media, we will cover online reviews in more detail later; however, we wanted to explain *why* you need to care about online reviews. To do this, let's step back for a moment and look at our behavior and the behavior of our friends and family. Think about the last time you purchased something online. Perhaps you went to Amazon and looked for a book or new electronic device. When you browsed the products, you likely took into account the number of stars an item had. You probably just skimmed the detailed description from the manufacturer or publisher and started reading the reviews. Even if a good friend recommended a book or product, you may have decided to buy something else once you went online and read the reviews. Similarly, many people check Yelp, Google, or even Angie's List before hiring a service.

When we discussed this topic at a CLE training we provided, an attorney chuckled, raised his hand, and admitted to a similar scenario. He said that he had a friend who had his carpets cleaned and seemed happy with the service. He asked for the name of the company and, after looking it up online, saw a number of negative reviews. As a result, the attorney ended up going with a different carpet cleaner. This is incredible. He saw the actual work product of the cleaner and received a recommendation from his friend, but online reviews from total strangers changed his opinion and behavior.

This behavior has not been lost on the search engines, either. When you use Google to search for phrases in which a product, local business, or local professional could be the possible answer, the search engine practically litters the results with review information: they are even showing up in Google AdWords now.

See *Figure 8*.

The importance of online reviews is illustrated not only by our own behavior and the behavior of search engines but also by supporting consumer studies. A 2014 study by BrightLocal found the following:

- 88 percent of consumers say that they read online reviews for local businesses (up from 85 percent in 2013).

- 67 percent of consumers read six reviews or fewer to make up their mind (down from 77 percent in 2013). This means that consumers are reading more reviews before they feel they can trust a business.

- 72 percent of consumers say that positive customer reviews make them trust a business more (as opposed to 73 percent in 2013).

- 88 percent of consumers trust online reviews as much as personal recommendations (a 10 percent increase from 2013).

The message is clear: consumers want to see online reviews for all kinds of professional services, including legal.

We will address online reviews and the appropriate strategies you need to follow later in this book.

Figure 8: Reviews frequently appear in search results.

- The Internet has led to a significant change in consumer behavior with regards to how consumers find a law firm.

- Referrals by word of mouth must be supported by a strong web presence: people go online to verify information and learn about your firm before they call.

- Unlike most forms of marketing, search engine marketing is not interrupt marketing. With interrupt marketing, the advertiser hopes that the prospect is in the perfect frame of mind to buy when a TV ad, billboard, direct mail piece, magazine advertisement, or even online banner ad is seen. With search, you know that someone is looking for an answer to a problem that you can solve.

- Search engines have made significant strides in attacking black hat tactics in the last two years. If you don't know how your web marketing or SEO firm is getting you top rankings and traffic, then you could be at risk.

- The fastest return on search engine marketing may be PPC; however, by utilizing a more long-term approach and properly managing your online presence in the search results, you will have a high ROI for years to come.

- The volume of people and the amount of time spent on social media platforms cannot be ignored. Your law firm needs to have a presence on these platforms. *Go where the people are.*

- Search engines are beginning to incorporate social media signals into their algorithms.

- Online reviews are extremely important, and people attribute as much credibility to online reviews as they do to a recommendation from a friend.

- Search engines are incorporating online reviews directly into the search results.

Chapter 2:

What Is Your Marketing Strategy?

Before we dive into our recommendations for managing your online presence, we want to take a second to talk about your marketing strategy. It is important to understand that we are not online marketing zealots who say that you should spend all of your time and effort marketing online, and online only. We are in the business of marketing when and where it makes the most impact on your law firm. But how do you know where your time is best spent?

We feel strongly that you need to have a comprehensive marketing strategy. Often, this means dividing your marketing investment across multiple channels. While declining in effectiveness, even the yellow pages might provide some return on investment for some law firms, depending on the target market. If you are making more from new business than you are paying, we aren't going to recommend that you stop a particular tactic. However, it is essential that you understand that the effectiveness of your marketing activities will change over time.

We help many firms work to understand which marketing activities are bringing them prospects. Whether you use manual forms, shared spreadsheets, or online tools, the key is to know how your prospects found your firm. In the work we have done with law firms, we have found that the most successful firms typically don't get a one-activity answer. Today, the answer goes more like this: "Well, Jim mentioned your name to me, then I noticed your name in the newspaper. So I visited your website and read some reviews online, and I feel that you are the right lawyer to help me out."

Even if someone says that he or she found you on Google, it is important to investigate further in order to find out if the prospect heard about your firm prior to that search. Frequently, your prospect will say something like, "Oh yeah, I saw your billboard but couldn't remember your name exactly, so I used Google to find you."

Answers like these tell us that having multiple marketing channels is very important and that having a strong web presence is crucial to supporting your other marketing channels. So, which marketing channels should you utilize? What works best? Well, to answer that, you need to dig a little deeper and answer some critical questions about your firm.

The Power of Your Brand

Branding is an area in which many law firms seem to fall short. Yet your law firm's brand is the starting point when determining your marketing strategy. Branding is so important that it is our first step in developing a comprehensive marketing plan for all law firms we work with—regardless of size, practice area, or current online presence.

Many lawyers and some marketing professionals (unfortunately) consider branding to be just their logo, business cards, and letterhead (and many agencies reinforce this misconception). However, branding is really about defining who you are and what makes your firm unique compared to other law firms in your community or market.

We are going to jump into how to uncover your brand in a minute; first, we need to explain why it is such a big deal.

Until you uncover your brand, you do not know how to communicate about your firm to your target client (something we walk through shortly). Because your brand identifies the various characteristics of your firm, the staff, the attorneys, and more, the brand acts as a guide for answering several difficult marketing questions. When you put the work into understanding your brand, it becomes easier to make decisions regarding your website design. As you walk through the process of improving your marketing, you can always ask yourself: "Based on our brand, what would the answer be?"

Understanding your brand also helps you dive into what separates your firm from the competition. Are you just another law firm? Or are you a firm that has a personality? Hopefully you feel that you are not just another law firm, but that your firm has characteristics that are unique.

In developing a brand, you will need to answer a lot of questions about yourself. Below is a questionnaire that you can use to start the conversation about your law firm's brand:

The following questions are not meant to be limiting or definitive. Don't hesitate to cut or adapt questions in a way that helps you communicate what is important about your firm. This is not a checklist but rather a guide to foster a beneficial conversation.

FIRM OVERVIEW

Provide a history of your firm.

- When was the firm founded?
- Who originally founded the firm? Is that person still present?
- What drove the founder(s) to start his or her own firm instead of joining an existing one?
- How large is your firm in total (attorneys, clerks, etc.)?
- Has your firm been involved in any well-known cases?
- Why should people be interested in your firm's history?

Describe your services.

- Force rank your top practice areas (up to six).
- Why did you rank them in this order (e.g., profitability, experience, frequency, interest)?

Identify your unique selling proposition.

- What does your firm do differently than your competitors?
- Do you see litigation as a last resort or a viable option from the start?
- Explain where you would like your firm to be in five years.
- Would you like more/fewer employees? More/fewer practice areas?

FIRM VALUES & BELIEFS

Explain the firm's values.

- What is your favorite part of being an attorney?
- What part of the legal process are you most passionate about? Why?
- What drew you to the legal profession?
- What aspect of your job do you most value?

Describe the firm's beliefs.

- What does your firm stand for?
- What does your firm stand against?
- What type of individual, case, or cause are you most excited to support, and why?
- Outside of daily office activities, what are you passionate about/ involved in (e.g., nonprofits, children's programs, education, sporting leagues)?
- What types of community organizations or local events are you or your firm involved in?

FIRM PERSONALITY

Describe the personality of the partners.

- How would you describe your office?
- How do your clients contact you?
- Do clients have 24/7 access to your firm? Can they reach you outside of office hours?
- Do you form more friendly or strictly professional relationships with clients?
- Do your clients refer to you by your first name or title?

Define the culture of the office.

- Describe a typical day in the office.

- How is your office designed and organized?
- What traits do/would you look for in new hires?

CLIENT EXPERIENCE

Outline the typical client process.

- Who manages all incoming calls (i.e., an office employee or an answering service)?
- Do you typically prefer to meet in person or over the phone? Why?
- Who is the first person a client meets when he or she comes to your office?
- How does this interaction progress?
- Do your clients interact mostly with attorneys or paralegals?
- How do you conclude a case?
- How do you encourage lasting relationships with your clients?
- Do you get a lot of referrals from other firms? What firm(s)?
- Is the client process different for a referral client?

Describe the client's perspective.

- What is a client feeling before meeting with you?
- How does your firm address those emotions?
- How does a client feel after meeting with you?
- Who typically contacts your firm (e.g., a family member or the person directly involved)?

CLIENT DEMOGRAPHICS

Describe your typical clients.

- Who is currently walking through your office door?

- Male or female? Age? Education level? Occupation? Income?
- Where would your typical client be more likely to shop: Walmart, Target, or Macy's?
- What events lead your clients to need an attorney?
- In your experience, what factors influence potential clients when choosing an attorney?

Define the ideal client.

- If you could clone a client, who would that client be? Why?
- What about that client makes him or her valuable?
- What is his or her age, gender, education level, and income?
- What type of car does he or she drive?
- Where does he or she shop?
- Is he or she married? Children?
- What types of social media does he or she most often use?

REGION AND CULTURE

Describe the geographical region that you serve.

- In what specific regions does your firm practice?
- What term(s) should be used to refer to the region(s)?
- Which nearby sports teams does your region favor? Is there a preferred sport in your region?
- Which nearby sports teams (college or professional) interest you?
- Are high school sports popular in your region?
- Are you near any well-known attractions, parks, or museums?
- If the Travel Channel or Food Network came to your region, where would they go?
- Is the history of your region important to its residents?
- What aspect of the history of your city is important to you?

Describe the culture of your region.

- How does this relate to your typical prospective client?
- What is the average education level in your region?
- What about your region makes you proud to live and work there?
- If you were to take me on a guided tour of your community, where would we go?

COMPETITION OVERVIEW

Identify online competitors.

- Your research online shows you are competing with:
- What should we know about these firms?
- Why would someone choose one of these firms over yours?
- What makes your firm better or different than these firms?

Identify local competitors.

- Which local firms are your greatest competition?
- What should we know about these firms?
- Why would someone choose one of these firms over yours?
- What makes your firm better or different than these firms?

VOICE AND TONE

- Describe your current website content (text, images, video, etc.).
- Who wrote the current content on your website?
- What do you like and dislike about your current content?
- How would you describe your social media presence (i.e., active, passive, nonexistent)?
- Why did you choose that approach?

- Define the voice of your website.
- From what point of view would you like your content to be written? (first person, third person, etc.)
- Describe the tone you would like to convey (e.g., personable, authoritative, relatable). Why did you choose this tone?
- Would you prefer to relate intellectually or emotionally with potential clients? Why?

VISUAL IDENTITY

Describe your current visual identity.

- Do you want to use your existing logo? Do you have other versions of your logo?
- Do you feel that your logo captures the personality of the firm? If yes, how so?
- What are the top three things you like about your current site?
- What aspects of your current site work well? Why?
- What are the top three frustrations you have concerning your current site?
- How do you feel your firm is currently represented online?

Establish your preferred visual identity.

- What colors are you drawn to?
- What sites, in or outside of your profession, do you like?
- What type of photography or illustration do you prefer? Can you provide examples?
- What websites do you spend most of your time on?
- What do you want your website to offer to potential clients?

As you can see, a fair amount of work goes into preparing for your branding exercise. Once you have this document completed, you should sit down in a conference room and discuss the questions and answers. If certain questions were difficult to answer, ask yourself why. Try to create a narrative about your firm.

In the end, you are looking for the following information to surface out of this exercise:

- What does your law firm stand for? Who are you?

- How would someone describe your firm based on the information in this questionnaire?

- Is there a certain type of client you prefer to work with, based on this exercise?

- Describe the emotional nature of your firm and how that may be conveyed in your marketing material.

- Is your current website, online presence, and marketing material clearly communicating your brand?

From here, you can start to move into the next elements of creating a strategic marketing plan.

Unique Selling Proposition (USP)

The most important component of your marketing strategy—which you should invest a significant amount of time discussing—is your firm's brand. Once you have this established, you need to define your unique selling proposition, or USP.

In almost every market and industry, it is important to differentiate yourself from the competition. Most likely, you compete with a number of law firms within a small radius of your office, many of which practice in the same areas of law. How does someone know that yours is the right firm for him or her? It is important to be able to define your USP and have all of your marketing pieces and client interactions support that message.

One thing that we often remind lawyers, especially those at small to medium-size law firms, is that it's hard to grow by competing on service quality alone. You need to change the conversation. Instead of shouting, "Hey, look at me! I am a great firm too," you want to confidently say, "We are all about [this]. We do things differently. If you're into [this], we're a great fit for you."

For example, let's look at FedEx. We may all use the United States Postal Service more frequently, but we know that when we absolutely, positively have to have a piece of mail delivered overnight, it's FedEx that deserves our money and trust. The company's marketing message, customer service, and technology used (really, everything they do) points to its unique selling proposition: being the most trusted overnight document carrier.

Note that FedEx doesn't claim to be the best delivery carrier overall; instead, the company differentiated itself by being the most trusted *overnight* carrier. The interesting thing about this brand message is that it actually alienates some potential customers. If you don't need to get a document somewhere fast, you probably won't consider paying $12 to mail it when a Forever stamp will do. But, FedEx has grown leaps and bounds by being targeted and unique.

Many law firms we meet have not even thought about their USP. To help them (and now you), we have created a number of questions designed to identify what makes a law firm different from the competition. The key questions that we start with are:

- What is unique about your firm?
- How is working with your firm different from working with other firms in the area?
- How would clients describe your firm?
- What are the specific needs your firm exists to address?
- What does your firm do to address these needs?
- What do you stand for? *or* What do you stand against?
- What personality do you put forth when someone experiences your brand (works with your firm)?
- What is your firm's promise to prospects?

After going through these questions, one lawyer told us that he realized that his firm was very successful at working with professional women who are going through a divorce. The firm set out to differentiate itself for that specific market. The firm's messaging, advertising, networking strategies, and website content all derived from that simple but important USP discovery.

What is your law firm's USP, and how is that shaping the way in which you reach and communicate to your prospects?

Persona Marketing: Demographic(s) of Your Best Clients

Once you have determined your USP, it is important to honestly define your ideal client demographic. Step back and think about your *best* clients. In the past couple of years, which types of clients have you preferred to work with? Look at what makes those types of clients unique.

Ask yourself the following questions:

- Who are your best prospects/clients?
- Are they mostly male or female or a mix of both?
- How old is your best client?
- Did they go to college?
- How much do they make in income?
- Where do they live?
- What kind of place do they own/rent?
- What kind of car do they drive?
- What are their beliefs/political affiliations?
- What social networks are they likely to use often?
- Is there anything unique about your best prospects/clients?

The firms that hone in on the differentiating points of their ideal client's demographic will actually have an easier time finding and marketing to this audience. They will also be able to more easily identify the right keywords to focus on for search engine marketing.

Remember that you can have more than one persona that you target. Maybe you work with a certain type of person in X practice of law but a completely different kind of person in Y practice of law.

Try to keep the number of personas you are targeting to two or three, maximum. It is tempting to target "everyone" or "these 15 types of people," but you should really try to identify your *best* target clients. If you are finding it too difficult to limit the number of personas to three, try broadening your definition. By stepping back a little, you will be able to lump multiple personas into groups, helping you boil down to two or three.

Creating a Marketing Strategy

If you take the time to create a clear picture of your brand, USP, and target persona, creating a marketing strategy becomes a lot easier. You will now be able to determine where your prospects spend time, how you would communicate to them about who you are, and what separates your law firm from your competition. Then you will just need to go out to those places and start adding value.

Maybe your clients are all on LinkedIn, or maybe they read *The New Yorker*. Either way, you should have some direction and targets to aim for. Your marketing mix can include a blend of traditional and digital. However, just because you *can* market somewhere does not mean you *should*.

The remainder of the book will walk through the online world of marketing. The words you use to describe what you do are at the crux of your online communication. Those are called "keywords."

The Right Keywords

Having a website is all well and good, but it doesn't do much for you if nobody sees it. You have to get Google to notice you and to rank you highly. But highly for what? In what searches should you invest your time, effort, and money in order to get ranked? This is why you need to think about your target keywords—an important concept to understand.

What are keywords, you ask? Keywords are the words (either one word or multiple words) that users type into Google's search box. A multiple-word keyword, like "commercial real estate attorney," "estate planning attorney," or even "how to pay for nursing home care with social security" is a "long-tail keyword" phrase. Users enter one of these keyword phrases into a search engine, such as Google, and the search engine displays what it thinks to be the most relevant websites (or answers) to that search.

That, in a nutshell, is the definition of a keyword. Within keywords, you will find two varieties: branded and non-branded.

Branded Keywords: Branded keywords are all the keywords that describe you, your brand, and your proprietary products. These include your firm name, your personal name, and the name of the products you sell. This is how people that are referred to your firm often find your information … by "Googling" you using your specific branded keywords.

For example, our firm could be called "The Law Offices of Homer & LeBret." "Homer & LeBret Law," "Mark Homer," and "Jabez LeBret" would also be branded keyword phrases for our firm.

When people go to Google and type in your firm name (or personal name), they are obviously looking for you. They might be doing research about you or looking for your phone number, address, or blog. The important thing to note is that they already know about you. This means that you do not need to—nor should you—spend much time or energy optimizing for branded keywords. When people specifically search for you on Google, the search engine should do a great job of ranking you on Page 1. Of course, this assumes that your website and web presence are set up correctly—something we will walk you through in later chapters.

It is important to know what information is tied to your name on the internet. When we Googled the name of one of our client's partners, they were appalled to discover that the fourth return on Page 1 of Google was "[Lawyer Name] child sex offender." You can imagine the look of horror on his face when we had to break this news to him. No, the attorney was not a sex offender; it was merely someone else who had the same name. We only bring this up to stress the importance of owning Page 1 for your name—or at least ensuring there is no disparaging information on the page. If there is, do not panic; just start building profiles and improving your web presence and you should be able to push that information off of Page 1 of Google.

Referrals are a strong driver of new business for many law firms. We often tell many lawyers to start their online strategy by focusing on their branded keywords to protect their referral business. We would hate to see you lose a referral you didn't even know you had because they were not able to find information about you online, or because the information online did not match the perceived referral.

Non-Branded Keywords: Non-branded keywords are all of the keywords, both short- and long-tail, that prospects use to find answers online. This includes phrases like "How long does alimony last?," "How do I get my license back after suspension?," or "criminal defense attorney."

These are the keyword phrases for which you want to optimize. (Further on in this chapter, we will discuss how to find the best keywords and where to use them.) This type of keyword drives your business outside of referrals. When you optimize for non-branded keywords, you are putting your website in front of people who do not yet know you and who are searching for the services that you offer. If you are an adoption attorney, you want to rank on the first page of search results for the phrase "adoption attorney" in your local area.

However, not all of your efforts should be focused on non-branded keywords. It is important that you protect your referral business and focus on *both* types of keywords.

Merely knowing the definition of a "keyword" is not enough. What keywords should you use? What keywords should you avoid? What keywords will get Google to notice that you are the best search result for a specific keyword phrase?

When we sit down with a law firm to discuss online marketing strategies, there are two mistakes we see nearly every time the conversation lands on keywords:

Law firms are often excited to show us that they rank first for their particular business name, like "Jones, Smith, & Carrier Partners LLC." So excited, in fact, that it's almost tough to tell them that it's nothing to be too excited about: you should rank high for your exact name with smart and moderate effort.

If users are searching for your firm name online, that's great news; it means they already know your firm and, hopefully, what your firm does. They've probably been reached by one of your other marketing techniques, or better yet, they were referred to your firm. Because of referrals, it is not a waste of time positioning your firm so that the people who already know you can find you. In fact, these efforts can drive up your business without imploring any other marketing methods. Typically, any bump in revenue you receive from properly securing your branded search terms will be small, but you never want to lose a referral because your web presence was not properly optimized for your branded keywords.

New clients are still very important. Don't forget: you're using the Internet to establish a professional reputation online and to get new customers. This means you need to present an attractive solution to anyone who has a problem, and this includes referrals.

Search, in its most basic sense, is a place where people find answers to problems. People need help with things like "buying out a business partner," "veteran's benefits," "long-term health care," "divorce advice," "car accident injury," "unfair reasons for being fired," or "real estate issues." These are the types of keyword phrases that people put into the search box everyday. New prospects are not typing in "Jones, Smith, & Partners LLC." They're typing in, "How do I get an estate plan?" or "Can I sue another company for violating a non-compete?" These are all issues for which a law firm may be able to provide a solution. You want to rank for these types of keywords.

Too often, we see law firms spending time, money, and effort to rank for terms that only make sense to someone who works in that particular profession. One such term is the keyword phrase "elder care law." Not many people know that elder care is an entire area of law. Though people might learn about this term and start searching for it in the future, they're not doing so in great numbers right now. What the ideal elder law prospect is searching for are phrases like "How can I afford long-term care?," "How can I afford a nursing home?," "How can I get veterans benefits?," or even "estate planning." People may not understand the terminology surrounding elder law, but there has been enough use of the term "estate planning" outside of legal circles that they think estate planning might be what they're looking for. What they're really looking for, however, is someone to help with VA benefits or Medicaid.

When selecting keywords, it is crucial to remember that you must look at keywords from the user's perspective. You should not expect users to search for terms that they may not be able to define. For example, don't go to your bar association for their definitions of keywords—unless it's to see which keywords *not* to use. It's a trap that people fall into all the time, and you've got to watch out for it. Even those of us in the marketing world are not immune. We deal in search and social media Internet marketing, and when we're not careful, we find ourselves using terms that people outside of the industry wouldn't use and don't care about: "SEO," "website optimization," or "SEM." These are terms that our clients would never type into a search box online. Instead, they would type something like "law firm marketing" or "How do I get my law firm to show up in Google search?" Those are the keywords that we as law firm marketers really care about.

These are the two biggest pitfalls in keyword selection, and they both stem from one thing: lack of knowledge—specifically, lack of awareness regarding what people search for. There are a number of tools available online to find out what people search for, including Google's Keyword Planner.

 BIG TIP

Just over a year ago, Google's free Keyword Tool was replaced by a new tool: Keyword Planner. While the tool was enhanced, it is no longer free. To access Keyword Planner, sign in to your AdWords account at **https://adwords.google.com**. Once you've signed in, find the **Tools and Analysis** menu. From there, click on "Keyword Planner." If you don't have an AdWords account, visit **http://www.google.com/adwords/** to sign up. You may be required to put a credit card down and pay a nominal fee to get access to this tool.

These various online tools are helpful, and those who know how to use them will certainly benefit from the services they provide. However, the best and possibly quickest way to start finding the right keywords is to simply ask your family and friends. Google is used by ordinary people, so ask your friends, family, and colleagues outside of the legal industry for help. Ask them to explain what your firm does as if they were telling a friend. They will use terms in plain English to describe your business, and those are the terms that ordinary people are going to type into the search box.

The reason that this method works is that it gets into the mind of a potential client. If you give a 60-second description of what you do to a client, and he or she turns around and tells that to a friend, it's not going to sound the same. In fact, it will likely be very different. What you're looking for in keyword selection is not how you describe your own business; it's how clients and prospects describe it. If you're not ranking for the keywords that people are using to search, nobody's going to find you.

BIG TIP

Once you've performed quick research with your family and friends, there are two other ways that you can gain insight into the keywords that people are really using on Google.

The first way is to use Google's Autocomplete feature, which can help you understand what people are searching for. If you go to Google's search box and start typing in one of your newly researched keywords in the form of a question, you will see a drop-down menu appear with suggestions to complete your search. The suggestions are given based on what people have recently been searching. Those suggestions can help you identify several other keyword phrases to use.

The second way is to perform a search with your keywords and then scroll to the bottom of your search results. You may see a section entitled "Searches related to [your keyword phrase]." This section contains other phrases that Google believes are similar to the keywords you entered into the search box. Some of those could serve as additional keyword phrases for your firm.

This might seem a little overwhelming, but don't worry. We're not saying that you have to nail this on the first try or that you can't change keywords over time. It's not the end of the world if you choose the wrong keyword on day one; keywords can be modified, refined, or even switched out altogether. Don't overthink your keyword selection to the point that you freeze. Start off by asking your neighbors and friends, as we described earlier, to find initial keywords. As you get more advanced, you can start using some of the tools we talked about to refine your keyword selection. (Those tools will definitely benefit you, but they're not essential right out of the gate.) Begin simply, and slowly grow in complexity as you master each step of the process.

Be cautious with keyword data. It is easy to draw unrealistic conclusions based on raw data. Just because people may be searching more for something does not always equal more clicks to your website. Often, the more a search term is being searched the higher the competition for that term.

You will need to think about two things: your traffic volume and your conversion percentage. Let's say that you only convert into clients 0.5 percent of people searching online in your geographic area. Now, add all your targeted keywords; this will give you an idea of new business possibilities online. Although a rudimentary way of figuring out your possible results, build a spreadsheet and start calculating your total return on traffic at a certain conversion rate. Feel free to email us your prediction; we would be happy to tell you if you are even in the ballpark in your area.

A well-planned campaign should get your firm ranked for at least three phrases, each with its own traffic numbers. By implementing the marketing and conversion strategies that we cover in the following chapters, you should see positive results.

 WARNING

Do not think that bigger is always better. This means that you should not believe that the more competitive keywords are always superior. Sometimes, it's better to start by going after an easily dominated keyword. Think long-term instead of flashy.

These kinds of results do not happen overnight—or even over the course of one month. In fact, you don't want them to happen that fast. You want the kind of online presence that produces great results over an extended period of time, not just one month and done. In order to produce these long-term results, you need to build an extensive, well-established online foundation—and that is what this entire book is about.

A pitfall that firms commonly succumb to is creating a URL with lots of keywords in the domain. This is an old SEO technique, commonly referred to as Exact Match Domain, or EMD.

Here's an example: let's say that you're an attorney in Dallas, Texas, and you've decided on the keyword phrase "estate planning attorney Dallas TX." A keyword-rich URL would be something like "**http://www.EstatePlanningAttorneyDallasTX. com**." This strategy used to help with ranking, but it no longer carries any weight. If you aren't tied to a URL (in other words, if you have not owned and optimized the keyword-rich URL for an extended period of time), we recommend that you create a URL with your firm name in it. A branded URL will be easier for people to remember and type free of error. This also helps them find your website again and refer your firm to others.

Do not panic if you already have a keyword-rich URL. While Google used to give more weight to exact match domains, that is no longer the case. That being said, having a keyword-rich URL will not necessarily hurt your rankings, especially if you are doing everything else right. Moreover, the effectiveness— or lack thereof—of this technique is still a point of contention in the industry.

This strategy is just one example of the way in which technology and online marketing change rapidly. Because of this, we want you to be as informed as possible. We recommend that you consult our blog regularly to stay on top of any other updates.

Niching

As you may have already guessed, you can't be highly ranked for every keyword in every practice area. Unless you're a general practice attorney in a small town, there will be a crowd of other attorneys vying for the same top spot for many different keywords. To stand out, you need to select some specialty or niche as your focus.

This isn't to say that you can't do other things or cross-sell once you get clients. However, you do have to step back and strategize when it comes to niching. Where is most of your revenue coming from? Where do you want it to come from? What is your most profitable set of clients? (These questions were discussed earlier when we talked about your USP and client personas.)

Some areas require a significant amount of a senior partner's time; others may be handled mostly by paralegals, with only a review by the senior partner. The second may be more profitable.

The big picture: to dominate online, you have to know where you want to go, then focus on those very few things. Choose something that you'd be happy with if 75 percent of your business came from that one thing. What is it? This area is where you should start with regards to your keywords. Dominating the search rankings in the areas of elder law, personal injury, estate planning, divorce, DUI, and so forth—all at once—is extremely difficult, if not outright impossible. Begin with the most important keyword: the niche that you want to own in the future. Dominating that one keyword phrase means owning that particular source of business in your area.

An extremely important aspect of this strategy is determining whether or not you're in an area where someone else is already dominating a larger keyword phrase. If another firm or attorney is dominating the keyword phrase that you want, you can always focus on smaller subsets of that phrase: if you can dominate two or three smaller keyword phrases, you may end up getting more business than the firm that went after the larger, broader term.

In keeping with our earlier elder care example, let's say you want to dominate the keyword "veteran's benefits."

Once you've narrowed down three to five keyword phrases, you'll want to make sure those phrases are included in your title tags. This is something you should ask your webmaster for help with. Note that the order is very important: you want the title tag to start with the keywords, then move into the location. Don't lead with your firm name; it's all over your website, and people (and Google) aren't going to miss it. Instead, start with the important keywords (and make sure that those are naturally interspersed all throughout your website). For example, a Portland estate planning attorney may have a title tag that reads "Estate Planning Attorney | Portland, OR | Smith & Smith LLC."

WARNING

Don't overdo it. Google is looking for real people with real content, not automatons who simply spew out keywords nonstop. There's a joke in the search engine optimization industry about this practice:

> Q: How many search engine experts does it take to change a light bulb?

> A: Light. Bulb. Light bulb. Lamp. Fluorescent. Incandescent. LED. Flashlight...

The joke is light-hearted, but the message is clear: don't saturate your website with keywords! Make sure that your keyword density (the number of keywords per one hundred words) hovers around 4 percent in the page text. Okay, we don't want to confuse you with terms like "keyword density," but now you know the specific data and can use it if you so choose. You can also simply stick with talking about your subject in a natural way, and your keyword usage will typically just work itself out.

All of the knowledge in this book is important for you to understand because it enables you to create your own online strategy—for keywords and beyond—or be savvy when hiring an agency to do it for you. If you hire an outside agency, you'll now be able to make sure that they are experts who will ask the tough questions and really help you create the right online strategy for your firm, as opposed to a webmaster who will put up a quick website without paying attention to anything else. There are lots of people trying to sell something quick and dirty instead of doing things the right way. Don't get fooled or go into any negotiations without knowing what an online marketing agency should provide you.

Once you've got your keywords and your domain name ready, it's time to step up your game by diving into advanced local search techniques.

- There are a lot of places where you can spend your marketing dollars. You need to think about your marketing strategy so that you spend them effectively.

- Define your unique selling proposition (USP). Use it in your marketing strategy to describe what makes you better and different than other law firms in your area.

- Determine who your ideal target clients are so you can understand how to best market to them online.

- A website won't do anything for your business if no one finds it.

- To get Google to rank your website highly—where you will be most visible to potential clients—you need to use the right keywords.

- Keywords are one-word or multiple-word phrases that users type into Google's search box (e.g., "car accident attorney"). Google returns the search results that it thinks best matches those keywords.

- If you rank for the keywords that nobody searches for, no one will find you.

- When choosing keywords that you want to rank for, remember that it's not really important to focus on ranking for your firm name. Also, remember that you don't want to rank for keywords using legal jargon, which the average person doesn't use.

- Choose your keywords from a user's perspective. Ask your friends and family how they would describe what you do. What are people searching for online, and how can your firm provide a solution to their questions and problems?

- Remember that the keywords you try to rank for can always be tweaked or swapped out altogether; they're not set in stone.

- You can't dominate every keyword. Sometimes, it's better to rank for a less competitive keyword or for a keyword in an area where you'd like to get more business.

- Use your keywords in your website's copy and title tags, but *don't* stuff your keywords into every nook and cranny of your website. Your use of keywords should be natural and readable. Remember that an actual human being is going to read your content, not just Google.

Chapter 3:

How to Build and Dominate Your
Local Online Presence

The consequences of not having a quality online presence are dire. Unfortunately, any business or firm with no Internet presence (or even a substandard one) is left out of the online consumer research process. Yes, people still often fulfill their online searches locally; however, if you don't come up when they're doing their research, you'll simply fly under their radar and lose their business to another firm that has a solid Internet presence.

Consider these statistics from the previously cited 2014 BrightLocal research report:

- Just 8 percent of consumers had *not* used the Internet to find a local business in the last 12 months.

- 39 percent of consumers said that they used the Internet to find a local business at least one time per month (up from 37 percent in 2013).

The danger of avoiding an online presence or having an ineffective presence is clear. But you've made it this far, so you're ready to start creating your local online presence.

Your Online Presence: Why You Should Focus on Local…Kind Of

There are actually tons of places on Google and other search engines where you can get ranked. There are paid advertisements (or PPC), national rankings, local rankings, social search rankings, and local organic rankings. So why do we talk about your local online presence and not just your online presence? Let's start by defining the difference between local and national searches.

In *Figure* 9, you can see exactly what we are talking about. The local search rankings are the lettered rankings that correspond with the map on the upper right.

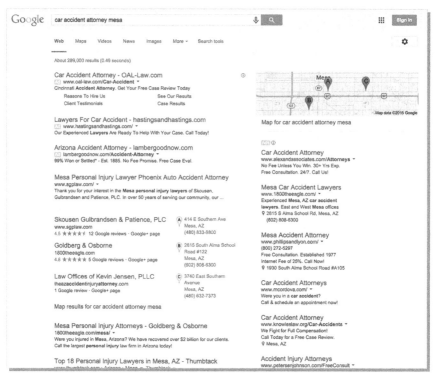

Figure 9: Local Google search returns

Around October 2010, we began to see this map appear on the main search results page. Over the past few years, Google has made some of the most significant changes to its search algorithm to date. One of these changes had major implications for searches that can be answered by finding a local brick-and-mortar business. The results of this type of search are local search returns, a feature that used to be available only on the Google Maps service. The next biggest impact came mid-2014 when there was a systematic removal of the long list of local returns in exchange for a shorter version—or none altogether. This provides a perfect example of why you never want to put all your online marketing eggs into one basket.

Because of recent changes, we have observed in many markets a dramatic shift in the layout of Page 1 of Google. We are going to walk you through several iterations of Page 1 results. Keep in mind that when you search on your own computer in your office, you may not be getting the same results as someone ten miles away.

The Google Maps local search return feature is very useful to both users and businesses, directing users to local businesses who provide the services they need and facilitating those businesses' offline conversion.

For a few years, Google was incorporating local search returns into its regular search page for almost all legal-related short keyword phrases, like "business contract attorney." Thanks to a change called "Universal Search," or blended search, a search for a brick-and-mortar business returned a map with up to seven marked locations, all local businesses. This change by Google made perfect sense. If someone is searching for a personal injury attorney in Denver, Colorado, they don't want to see results for attorneys in Charlotte, North Carolina. Users mostly want to find businesses located near their location. Also in this update, Google added a feature that automatically determines the user's location when he or she searches on Google.com.

Now, for unknown reasons, there is a mixed return depending on where you are located, the type of search you are doing, and the day you are searching. Yes, that makes people like us want to pull our hair out. The fact is, we are never certain what Google is going to do next, and we have a whole team of people that are very good at this. So, in the meantime, we are going to focus on both local and organic returns.

This uncertainty is bad news for law firms because there is now a real chance for competition on multiple fronts. Several years ago, local businesses simply couldn't compete on a national level with giants like Amazon and Wikipedia. It took companies like FindLaw and Lawyers.com to build up national search relevance and then sell that traffic to local law firms (for a significant fee). With the mixed results we are seeing, both local firms and national companies like Avvo and FindLaw will need to work hard to land on Page 1 of rankings.

Your firm can show up in the top three results on a local search page, often above any of the old standard search results. Applying the information in this book will help establish your firm on the map, specifically so that people in your community find your firm on the first page of Google when they search for your services. This will likely increase the amount of prospects calling and emailing your practice on a weekly basis—as long as you set things up properly, which we will discuss at length later.

Remember, there are plenty of other firms vying for these same spots, and just having a website isn't going to get you anywhere. (In fact, doing this process poorly can ensure that you never see the front page of Google at all). But, if you do a good job, are careful, and follow all the instructions in this book, you'll have a shot at hitting the A, B, or C spot in local search returns for your keywords.

If you are lucky enough to have a full 7-Pack of local returns, here is what you can expect. The following image, courtesy of Moz and Mediative[2], shows where people's eyes first move when they are given a search return on Google. What is important about this study is the fact that people immediately look at the local search returns. In this heat map, the search term used was "small boutique hotel in 'New Orleans'"—something that, though very different than your law practice, is also a local search.

See *Figure 10*.

The statistics concerning local search returns are astounding. Some in the marketing community say this may explain the departure from displaying local results on Google's part. Returns in the A, B, and C slots in the main search area garner more clicks than the rest of the page entirely. Since Google's revenue is connected to people clicking on ads, the search engine seems motivated to at least dial back the number of local searches. As you can see from the graphic, people avoid the ads almost completely and skip right over the national organic search returns. They also don't look at the map very often. Most people searching go straight to the A return without even thinking about it. Regardless, being on Page 1 of Google is essential.

Let's Get Local: Local Search Techniques

If you've been following this book thus far, you understand the importance of being found online, you have your marketing strategy and USP, and you have a strong sense of the keywords you are targeting. In fact, you're likely better off than anyone who has simply thrown together a website without

---

2   http://moz.com/blog/eye-tracking-in-2014-how-users-view-and-interact-with-todays-google-serps
     http://pages.mediative.com/SERP-Research

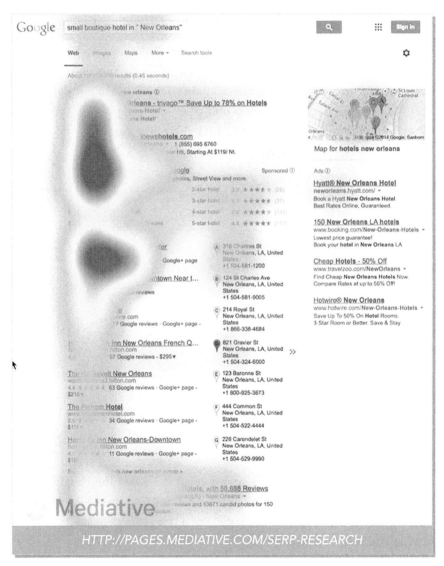

Figure 10: Moz eye-tracking heatmap

understanding these things, and you're definitely better off than anyone who has refused to transition to web-based marketing.

In the rest of this chapter, we're going to help you figure out how to make your firm a big-time local business on the web by using several advanced local search techniques.

For most law firms in the average city, Google will show your listing on searches performed within a 25-mile radius of your office location. This means that you can appear in search results on a prospect's computer up to 25 miles away from your office. However, this isn't always the case. In more densely populated cities, that radius shrinks significantly.

BIG TIP

When you search for your firm on your own computer, you will get skewed results because you visit your website more often than your prospects. Google pays attention to what you search and, if you search your own firm often, will return your website higher in search returns than it actually appears to someone else in your own city. Also, searching from outside your city location will skew your results. If you want to know where you rank locally, you should have someone you know who lives in your city and has never visited your website search for your keywords. From this search, you will see where you truly rank.

Take Seattle, for example. We have a client located in the Ballard area of Seattle. The firm's address to the office is Seattle, and if you asked the attorneys, they would tell you they work in Seattle. But if you are from Seattle, you know that Ballard is its own place.

Google also considers Ballard to be a unique location. You can actually set your city location in your search to be "Ballard, Seattle, WA" and get returns for that exact area. This is important for anyone in a larger city, like Chicago, San Francisco, Denver, Boston, New York, Miami, etc.

Your first goal should be to get your firm ranked in your exact location. Try searching on Google with your actual location, like Lincoln Park, Chicago, IL, and see if the results vary when compared to a search in Chicago, IL. If they do, you now know that there is a micro-location in the larger city.

After you've established that there is a smaller location in the larger area, begin adding your neighborhood name to your keywords. This will help Google to narrow down exactly where you are.

Getting Ranked in Your Local City or Another City

"I want to rank in my city and the city right next to me." That is a statement we get all the time from firms looking to us for help with ranking. So what have Google and all the other search engines said about your location with regard to getting ranked?

You are supposed to establish your web presence and pursue rankings in your actual physical location. Imagine if I were to call 411 directory information and ask for your address. What address would they give me? That is the address that Google wants you to use, and it is the address by which the search engine will rank you.

For some firms, it is very important to rank in cities other than their physical location. Here is a simple (and pretty much the only) work-around to this location conundrum: rent a temporary office space in another city. You cannot rent a P.O. box or use a shared mailbox drop, even if that box gives you a suite number. Google knows that The UPS Store is not a real office; trust us, do not try to fool Google.

If this seems unfair, remember that Google is trying to allow real businesses to get ranked in their local city. This is a great thing for your firm. If anyone could get ranked without having a real office space, then law firms from outside your city would game the system, dominate the rankings, collect all the leads, and sell those leads. This type of behavior used to happen; in fact, it even happened in the legal industry. Companies would rank highly on local search terms, make prospects fill out online forms, and sell those leads to attorneys. Google decided to cut out the middleman and let the prospect go directly to you.

Core Components to Getting Ranked Locally

Where do you need to focus to get ranked locally? You should focus your attention on: website optimization, directory services, links, reviews, and local city pages on your website.

Directory Listings: How to Set Up Your Listings, What Listings You Should Use, and What Listings You Should Avoid

If you read the first or second edition of our book, you may remember the good old days when you could rank highly by merely having a ton of directory listings. Well, those days are over. Gone. Kaput.

That doesn't mean, however, that directory listings are no longer important. In fact, they are super important. Now, you need to be even more vigilant about your directory listings and do a lot more online to get the results most firms want.

But first of all, what is a directory listing? If you've been an Internet user since the pre-search days, you are probably familiar with them. Directory listings are, in short, the online version of the yellow pages, and they list your business name, address, and phone number. Sites like SuperPages.com, YellowPages.com, Yahoo! Local, FindLaw, Super Lawyers, Avvo, Bing Local, and Google+ Local are all examples of directory listings. These listings are commonly called "citations" by those in the online marketing and search marketing industry.

There are hundreds, if not thousands, of directory listing websites across the Internet; however, there are 12 to 15 major websites on which you want to be listed. In addition to the main directories like MerchantCircle.com, SuperPages.com, Yelp, and Yahoo! Local, attorneys should be sure to get listed on legal-specific directories, like Avvo.com. Certain directories, like Infogroup, are more influential than others because they serve as sources of information. In time, as other directories use the information listed there, your information will proliferate all over the Internet. Because your firm's information will often spread from one directory to another, it is crucial to make sure that this information is correct and optimized in the most important and influential directories.

These directories have risen in prominence since Google moved its local search returns to the main page using Google+ Local. Even though we are seeing a sizable decrease in the importance of having a large volume of citations, your law firm still needs to have a fair amount of important listings that are done correctly.

The algorithm that determines which Google+ Local business listings belong on Page 1 of Google's search results takes a great deal of its ranking consideration from directory listings around the web. If you have 10, 15, or 35 directory listings, that looks very good to Google's ranking system. If your listings have reviews, that is even better. We'll get to reviews in the next chapter, but for now, it is sufficient to say that directory listings with reviews are very helpful. If your competition is getting more reviews than you, you often won't make the first page—they will.

How to List Your Law Firm

It's important to note that doing this wrong can *ruin* your online presence and overall strategy—so pay close attention.

You want your firm to be listed in a decent number of directories. There are some services out there that will do this automatically for you. More often than not, however, these automatic services are pretty spotty, and they oftentimes list you incorrectly. Because of this, you should add your firm's listings manually.

Listing your firm is a pretty easy, though time-consuming, process. To add a listing for your law firm, you simply have to go to directories and enter in your firm's information, photos, and description.

A majority of directory listing websites allow for a free listing. Some directory websites will try to upsell you with different services once you've added your free listing, but a paid listing is typically not necessary. In our experience, free listings optimized with the location and keywords are more than enough to bump a firm up to the top. We've had many clients—who never paid for directory listings—achieve top rankings on Google. You will most likely never need to pay for a directory listing, or any extra services. That is not to say that these additional paid services won't provide more traffic and clients to your business, but you don't need to start there. Instead, register with all the free ones first.

Law firms are particularly vulnerable to one of the most disastrous citation issues that can happen to a business: duplicate listings.

Quite frequently in a law office, there are three to four attorneys that comprise one office partnership. Sometimes, the attorneys will create their own listings, so the firm ends up with multiple listings for each attorney and one (or more) for the office as a whole. When Google queries the directory listings, it gets confused by the multiple entries for one address. The algorithm thinks that the duplicates are an attempt to game the system. As a result, it may ignore them all or display one partner consistently instead of the firm as a whole.

You want to ensure that you have only one listing for your firm and one listing for each attorney. In fact, it's better not to have individual listings for each attorney at the firm. That way, if an attorney ever leaves, you don't have to scour the Internet to delete listings associating him or her with your firm. If you already have listings for each practitioner, however, don't panic. Delete them if you can, and if you can't, edit and optimize them as you would any other listing.

How do you know if you have duplicate listings? Search for your firm's name, address, or phone number. In addition, search for your name and the names of the other people in the office. You should search via Google, naturally, but you should also search directly on many of the directory websites. If you do have multiple listings, delete them all except one.

Shady SEO companies used to try to trick search engines into boosting a website's rankings by creating duplicate listings. Now, Google cracks down on this practice. Remember that duplicate listings are harmful to your ranking! If your firm has too many duplicates, your ranking will suffer. Be very wary of this, and make sure to find and delete duplicate listings!

This is the reason that you need to be careful about a service that claims to automatically add you to 20 (or even hundreds of) directories. A few of these services work, but many others will simply add duplicate listings, which can ruin your whole presence.

After you have a baseline for your online success, you can opt for a paid enhancement to a directory listing and test its impact on the number of leads you receive. This way, you can measure the real cost and benefit of the investment.

You should be prepared for multiple phone calls from directories looking to sell you service add-ons. Changes to Google and other online advertising venues have left many of these directories scrambling to rethink their business models. Paying for a directory listing is no longer as necessary as it used to be, so resist the urge to listen to these calls and emails. It's just not necessary to pay for all of their extra services in order to see results.**

Another important thing to remember when you're creating directory listings is to use your keywords and location only in the description field given in the listing. Do not add keywords to your firm name. Google considers this practice to be spammy and will penalize businesses that include keywords and locations in their business name.

This can be used to your advantage, depending on your dedication to the strategy of adding keywords and your state's ethical guidelines. Some of our sharper clients have actually changed their legal business name to include their keywords and location (e.g., "Elder Law of Georgia Firm"). (This may remind you of the yellow pages game of putting *a*'s in business names to get to the top of the listings, like "A Great Dentist in Dallas, Texas.")

Note that Google doesn't penalize a business whose name officially contains its keywords or location. What the search engine watches out for is obvious keyword stuffing, or phrases like "Jones, Smith & Barney Attorneys at Law - Estate Planning - Elder Law - VA Benefits - Dallas, TX" in a business name. This is bad practice: those keywords should go in your description, not your business name.

When creating your listings, use your official firm name, both for ethical reasons and your online results.

Mike Ramsey, founder of Nifty Law, displayed the following warning clearly in a presentation at Avvo's Lawyernomics last spring. It went like this:

Your business listing in one place reads:

Smith, Homer, and LeBret LLP
1775 Mentor Road Suite 302
Cincinnati, OH 45212
513-444-2016

In another place, your business listing reads as follows:

Smith, Homer, & LeBret LLP
1775 Mentor Rd #302
Cincinnati, OH 45212
1-800-CALL-SHLL

When the search engines go to verify your authenticity and trustworthiness online, they take a look across multiple directory listings and validation resources.

To a search engine, these two listings look like this:

Smith, Homer, and LeBret LLP
1775 Mentor Road Suite 302
Cincinnati, OH 45212
513-444-2016

If the directory listing has suggested keywords, consider using them. They probably look very similar to the yellow pages categories that you are used to seeing. Some directory listing services allow you to type in your own keywords, in which case you should do so. Don't go crazy with the keywords, however. Google only values about three to four keywords—anything after that is considered to be gaming the system, and you will be ignored.

WARNING

The information on every directory listing must identically match the information on your website, other directory websites, and 411. Some companies will try to sell you tracking numbers that forward to your office phone, as they are a great way to measure how many people call you from your website or Google+ Local page.

Be very careful! Using tracking numbers incorrectly can hurt your local search presence.

As a firm that always has to show our clients their return on investment, we wish that tracking numbers could be used in directory listings. The issue is that the tracking number on your directory listing will not match the number in 411 and will be extremely hard to clean up if you change the tracking number.

Also, don't just replace the phone number on your website with your tracking number. When Google and other search engines try to validate your phone number, they often reach out to 411 data aggregator services, like Infogroup and Localeze. Google will crawl the web, trying to validate your business, and it will find your tracking number in one place and your real number in another. When this happens, Google will get confused and drop you in the rankings. We have witnessed this firsthand with clients who previously had tracking numbers. Companies like YP.com and FindLaw will tell you otherwise, but they are flat out wrong.

On your website, you can use a tracking number to see if someone visited your website from an organic search or from some other online referral. However, this has to be done very carefully. If someone goes directly to your website, the main number on your website should match the number in the directory listings and 411. However, you can utilize some coding tricks that will change your phone number to the tracking phone number if someone visits from a search engine or another website you want to track.

Every listing should have the same firm name, address, and phone number. The only thing that can vary from one listing to the next is your firm's description. Having listings that do not match your website and information is a sure way to guarantee that your competition will pass you in the rankings or, worse, that you will end up on page 39, trying to claw your way back to the first page.

There are a ton of directory sites. Some are better than others, and to be fair, they change from time to time. For a current listing of the top directories that many experts follow, visit the Get Listed Local Search Ecosystems graphics, located here: **http://moz.com/blog/2013-local-search-ecosystems**.

Earlier in the book, we mentioned that Google uses links to your website as an indicator of the value of your website. Think of directory listings as additional links. Directory listings are not the only links you can have pointing back to your website. To get results, you will still need links with stronger page authority and .edu and .gov links, in addition to your directory listings.

The more vigorous the verification step during the listing creation process, the better the value of the link. For example, Yelp, Yahoo! Local, and other directory listing websites will require that you receive a phone call from the directory service to your business phone in order to verify the listing. This means that someone has to be in your office answering the phone. That way, the directory service knows that the number is real. (Note that if you have an automated or outsourced phone service monitoring that phone line, you will have to disable it during the directory listing verification process.) Other directories may require that you live in a certain area and are verified by a person.

Listings like Avvo and those from the local chamber of commerce, local bar association, and the Better Business Bureau are often great directory listings and high-quality links back to your website. We typically recommend paying for membership to your local chamber of commerce and the Better Business Bureau. Not only do you get to display the badge on your website, but you also get to control a high-quality link.

Google+ Local: Your Most Important Listing

Your Google+ Local listing is extremely important. In fact, it may be the most important citation you create; be very careful when creating and editing it.

Unfortunately, Google+ Local is not as straightforward as it should be, due in large part to a number of changes made to the service by Google. Great strides were made this past year that simplified things for many businesses. However, it is still a confusing process for many business owners.

On Google, there are two types of pages that you need to differentiate between: Google Places listings and Google+ Local pages. (These listings do not have different official names, but we will assign them distinct names to clear up some of the confusion.)

The first type of page, the Google Places listing, has a map at the top of the page. It does not have a cover photo, verification checkmark, follow button, or any social features. The page has only two tabs, "About" and "Photos," and the description is limited to two hundred characters.

The second type of page, the Google+ Local page, has a cover photo, verification checkmark, follow button, and social features. The page has four tabs: "About," "Posts," "Photos," and "YouTube." There is a limit of five thousand characters on the description. See *Figure 11 & Figure 12.*

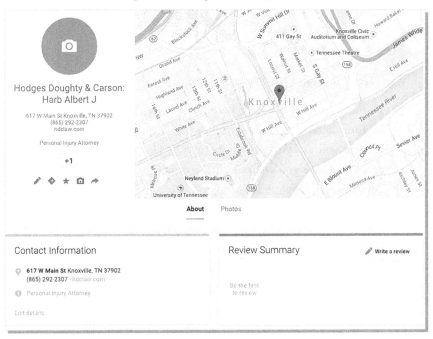

Figure 11: Example of a Google Places listing

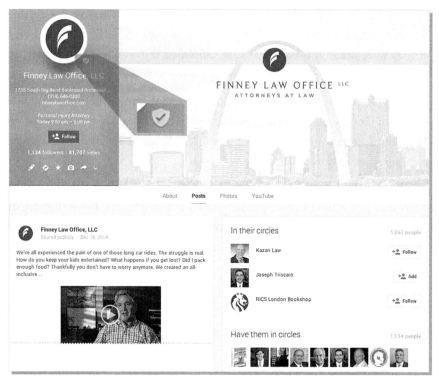

Figure 12: : Example of a Google+ Local page

Your goal should be to have a Google+ Local page. But how do you get there?

- If your firm **does not** have a Google Places listing, you can create one by going here: http://www.google.com/business/placesforbusiness/. Google will ask you to sign in to your Google account or create an account. Once you've done this, you will be instructed to search for your business. If your firm does not show up in the search, you should select "No, these are not my businesses." You can then fill in your firm's information, including its name, address, phone number, and category. As a final step, Google requires you to verify your firm by phone or by postcard to make sure that the business is real. When you've completed all of these steps, you'll be able to add more information about your firm and manage your listing.

- If you have a Google Places listing for your firm but you haven't claimed it, you should follow the same steps as before. However, when you search for your business, it should appear. Then, you should select it and go through the same verification process.

After you've claimed your Google Places listing, you can automatically create a Google+ Business page by logging into your Google Places account, going to your listing, and scrolling down to the "Google+ page" section. When you click "Start now" in this section, Google will automatically create a Google+ Business page for your firm and will "merge" your local Places listing with your Google+ page. (Lucky for you, Google has made the process a lot easier than it was before.)

The result is a verified Google+ Local page. Congratulations!

If, however, your firm has already claimed your Google Places listing, then things might get a bit more tricky.

If your listing is still in the old Google Places dashboard, you won't have the option to create a Google+ Business page automatically. Instead, you'll have to do it manually and go through verification again to merge your Places listing and Google+ page into one Google+ Local page. (Similarly, if you have claimed your Google Places listing and already have a separate Google+ Business page, you will have to go through the verification process again to merge the two pages, no matter which version of the Google Places dashboard you have.)

To create your Google+ Business page, go here: http://www.google.com/+/business/. When creating a Google+ Business page, it is absolutely *essential* that the category of your page be "Local Business or Place." If you do not choose this option, you will not be able to combine your Places listing and Business page. Similarly, if you have claimed your Google Places listing and already have a separate local Google+ Business page, you will have to go through the verification process again to merge the two pages.

We've found that this process can get complicated, and it's often necessary to call Google's support team for help. Finally, after you've created your listing, it is very important that you manage it in the right place. Once you have a Google+ Local listing, you should be making any edits to the listing from your Google+ account, *not* from Google Places.

Unfortunately, Google doesn't make it any easier for business owners; in fact, it changed its dashboard at least three times in 2013 alone. We recommend that you visit our blog for the latest information on Google+ Local.

If you haven't already created it yet, your Google+ Local page should be one of the last directory listings that you create. Set up about 15 to 20 other directory listings first, wait a week or so or until you have verified these listings, and then create your Google+ Local page.

Why wait? Well, when you create a Google+ Local page, Google goes forth and looks for information about your firm: directory listings, blogs, reviews, and so forth. If you've done all of the things we've talked about, you should rocket up to the top of the list once you create your Google+ Local page. If you want to be on the first page of Google's search returns, waiting those few weeks to make a Google+ Local page makes a huge difference in your ranking.

With the blending of Google+ and Google Places, the overall layout of Google's listings has changed significantly. Google makes updates to the layout and features of its listings frequently, so it is important that you check your Google+ Local listing regularly. Make sure that all of your information is unchanged and that the images are properly sized.

Here are the components that you should add to your Google+ Local page:

- **Firm information:** Make sure to add your firm's name, address, phone number, website URL, and hours of operation.

- **Images of your firm:** Your images should be good quality, properly sized, and attractive to potential clients. Google currently lets you add a profile photo and cover photo. Your profile photo could be your logo, for example, and your cover photo could be a photo of your office or of the members of the firm. Make sure not to leave any image spaces blank.

- **Description of your practice:** Add a compelling, optimized description of your firm. This should include how clients can benefit from working with you and what you practice. Of course, your description should also include your keywords, location, and firm name.

- **Categories:** Add your categories (e.g., "Lawyer" or "Divorce Attorney"). You cannot create custom categories, unfortunately. Google now requires you to select from its list of categories.

- **Reviews:** Ask satisfied clients to review your firm on Google+ Local. Do *not* review your own firm or fake reviews from clients. Getting reviews is so important that we have an entire chapter dedicated to the topic (coming up next).

- **Videos:** Make sure that any videos you upload to YouTube are created under the same Google+ user as the one that manages your Google+ Local Page.

Advanced Citation Tactics

Any listing that contains your name, address, phone number (or NAP), and URL is a valid citation. We used to reserve the following advanced information for our clients, but it is important to us to not withhold information, so we are adding it to this version of the book.

In your local town, there are a number of quality citations that get missed all the time. These are sponsorship citations. Your firm likely already sponsors one or more non-profit, school sports team, or other local organization, many of which have websites. Often, they will add the information and links of their sponsors to their websites. In particular, links from websites that end in ".edu" can be valuable. It is widely believed by many in the SEO community that links from websites that end in ".edu" are valued highly by search engines because they are strictly controlled. This is an opportunity for a natural, quality citation that you shouldn't overlook.

In addition, a sponsorship can increase goodwill in your community, better your firm's reputation, spread awareness of your firm, and serve as a topic for a local blog post (discussed later). If you sponsor the local high school football team, for example, you may get not only a link on the team's website but also a mention in the program passed out at all the games and on a sign at the field.

You should maximize any sponsorships in which you currently participate. In the future, be sure to ask any sponsorship solicitors if the sponsorship will include a place on the organization's website where you can have your name, address, phone number, description, and link to your website.

Another quality sponsorship-style link can come from offering a local scholarship. If you can do this in conjunction with a local university or high school, you have another opportunity for a link to your website. Moreover, offering a scholarship gives you the chance to encourage social sharing. Scholarships are frequently shared on social media. If you put the qualifications and instructions to apply on your website, this can lead to a lot of social signals as the link is shared among high school students and parents. These benefits come in addition to the traditional goodwill achieved in the community and a potential legitimate press mention in your local city paper.

Monitor Your Directory Listings

One mistake that many law firms make is that they spend the time and resources to create 30 or more directory listings and then never look at them again.

Unfortunately, in an attempt to make money on ad revenue, many small directory listing websites utilize old black hat methods to create large directory listing sites. They will use web bots to scour the Internet and collect data from other sites. Often, this data is scraped poorly, which results in bad data on the new site. Because of this, we recommend that you search your name, phone number, and address every couple of months. See if you are showing up in additional directories. If you are, make sure that they have all of your information correct, including your description and categories. If something is incorrect, you can typically submit your changes via a form or email. Some of these sites will never fix the problem, but others will take the time to fix your listing.

Press Releases

Directory listings are not the only web presence links that we have recommended. In the past, we recommended submitting press releases using a paid service in order to get your information to a number of online and real news outlets around the country. Press releases used to be a very powerful tool in getting ranked online. In the last couple of years, however, they have become almost worthless as a web presence strategy. This is because black hat companies took advantage of the system and started spamming the Internet with press releases every day.

14 GREAT PRESS RELEASE IDEAS:

1. Someone in your firm is speaking at an industry conference, local chamber, rotary club, etc.

2. You hire someone new into your firm.

3. Someone is promoted.

4. You join an association (local or national).

5. You start offering a new service.

6. You move into a new office space or add an additional office.

7. You have a successful client.

8. You receive an award or recognition from a local or national industry or association.

9. An employee of the firm is named to a charity benefit or non-profit board.

10. You sponsor a charity benefit, local sports team, or other organization.

11. You offer a scholarship for college students.

12. You are awarded a new business contract.

13. Your services tie into a current important news item (new government law, health discovery, tax time, etc.)

14. You launch a new website.

While we still recommend that you create press releases, we no longer advise you to submit them for syndication every time. Instead, you can create an "In the News" section on your website and add your press releases there. This is a good way to add to your website content. You should try to create a press release to put on your website about once every six weeks. If you do have a very important release that you feel could get picked up and shared by media outlets, consider utilizing a higher-end press release syndication service like PR Newswire. Note that, when syndicating, you get what you pay for. Free submission tools get you as much as you paid for them: zero. The more your story gets out there, the greater the possibility that it could get picked up (it *can* happen). A local paper could see the press release and pick up the story, for example.

It's important to note that press releases will naturally be shared and reposted all over the Internet. This is one case in which you are allowed to have duplicate content. In fact, big names—like The Associated Press and Reuters—even source duplicate content.

There is always a reason to create a press release. Because many attorneys get hung up on what to write about, here are some ideas for press release topics:

The Structure of a Press Release:

There is a certain way that you are supposed to write a press release, with a number of rules that you have to follow. Press releases are designed to disseminate information or notices regarding what's going on in the world. This is not the platform to talk about how awesome you are or to pitch your services.

Here is the basic structure of a press release: See *Figure 13*.

Firm Logo

Contact: Joe Smith
Tel: 555-555-5555
Email: Joe@SmithandSmith.com

FOR IMMEDIATE RELEASE
THE MAIN TITLE OF A PRESS RELEASE SHOULD BE
UPPERCASE AND CENTERED

The Subtitle Is Also Centered and Should Be Title Case

This is the summary body of the press release. It should include paragraphs that outline what the news concerns and why it is important.

This is the body of the press release. Include quotes from people, who can be people at your firm or people that were quoted in other media outlets, regarding the specific topic of your press release. This is the body of the press release. Include quotes from people, who can be people at your firm or people that were quoted in other media outlets, regarding the specific topic of your press release.

This is the body of the press release. Include quotes from people, who can be people at your firm or people that were quoted in other media outlets, regarding the specific topic of your press release. This is the body of the press release. Include quotes from people, who can be people at your firm or people that were quoted in other media outlets, regarding the specific topic of your press release.

The concluding statement goes here and should be no more than one or two sentences. The concluding statement goes here and should be no more than one or two sentences.

Your boilerplate (or who you are) goes here. Your boilerplate (or who you are) goes here.

#####

If you'd like more information about this topic or would like to schedule a media appearance with Joe Smith, please call Jane Doe at 555-555-5555 or email Jane@smithandsmith.com.

Figure 13: Press release template

- It is important—and to your benefit—to differentiate between your *local* online presence and your online presence.

- Google has structured local search returns so that they catch the eye of the searcher more than other elements in the search results.

- Directory listings, or citations, are the online version of the yellow pages. They include your firm's name, phone number, and address.

- There are hundreds of directory listings, but you don't need to be listed in *all* of them. Major directory sites where you should be listed include Google+ Local, Yahoo! Local, Yelp, YellowPages.com, and Avvo.

- The information that you put in each citation will proliferate all over the web, so make sure that everything you include is correct, optimized, and consistent with your website's information.

- Manually—not automatically—creating citations is the best way to ensure that your information is correct.

- Be very careful that you do not have duplicate or incorrect listings. Google's algorithm will be confused by the incorrect information and *will* penalize you by dropping your website's ranking.

- Use keywords in each citation—but do so carefully. Don't stuff in keywords where they don't belong, particularly in your business name.

- Don't use tracking numbers. These numbers won't match your firm's phone number and will confuse Google, leading to a drop in rankings.

- Your Google+ Local page is the most important listing you have. Be sure to add your firm's contact information, description, images, keywords, video, and reviews.

- You don't need to pay for citations. Create all the free ones first, and if paid listings are right for your firm, then continue to those.

- Press releases, while important for traditional reasons, do not provide the search value that they did just one year ago.

Chapter 4:

Everyone Trusts Strangers Now: Why Reviews Matter

We mentioned earlier that people may find you from an online review site or a Google search that returned your firm. Remember the data from the BrightLocal study we talked about before?

- 88 percent of consumers say that they read online reviews for local businesses (up from 85 percent in 2013).

- 67 percent of consumers read six reviews or fewer to make up their mind (down from 77 percent in 2013). This means consumers increasingly feel the need to read more reviews before they can trust a local business.

- 72 percent of consumers say positive customer reviews make them trust a business more.

- 88 percent of consumers trust online reviews as much as personal recommendations (up from 79 percent in 2013).

Even after learning this data, many people are confused by this part of the process, especially because clients create reviews. How can reviews from a third party make or break a search engine ranking? Certainly, they might be helpful to prospects reading what other clients have said, but surely they can't influence Google's monstrous ranking machine in your favor…can they?

As it turns out, they can and do influence the ranking system. Very much so, in fact: Google uses reviews in order to judge the validity of the business in question. Put simply, if the location has been reviewed, someone's been there. In addition, the review comments give an indication of the quality of the location, or whether it deserves to be ranked higher or lower. Many review sites allow reviewers to give star ratings, which are even more influential; Google actually scrapes these reviews from other sites to do a sort of website litmus test—a judgment of whether or not the establishment is viewed positively or negatively overall.

The importance of reviews cannot be overstated. In fact, Google recently made adjustments to incorporate and highlight online reviews in its search engine results pages even more. If you get as few as five reviews on your Google+ Local page, your listing will appear with a review ranking and star rating right in Google's search engine results page. If someone clicks on the reviews, Google now opens a pop-up window with the reviews—instead of taking you to the Google+ Local page or to the company's website. This is one of only a few times when you will you click on a Google search result and be redirected to something other than a website.

See *Figure 14* & *Figure 15*.

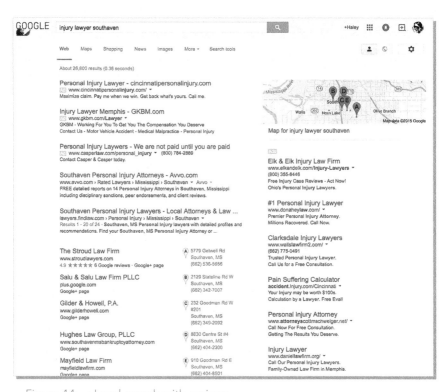

Figure 14: : Local search with reviews

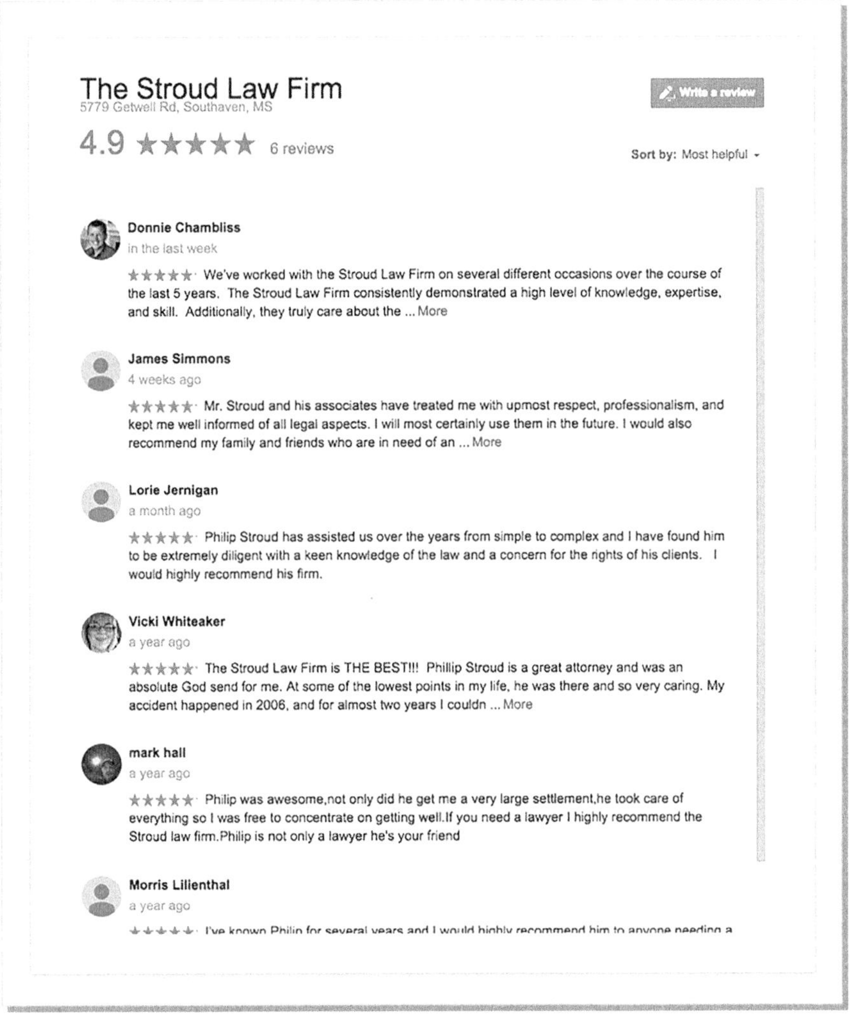

Figure 15: Google reviews appear in a pop-up over search results.

Furthermore, The Google+ Local page user interface now prominently displays the review section just below the description of your firm. Text saying "Write a review" or "Be the first to leave a review" specifically encourages users to give a review directly on the page.

See *Figure 16.*

Figure 16: Google+ Local page encourages people to write a review

Google uses reviews to determine whether or not you're the best solution to the problem the user is trying to solve. This is critical because the whole premise of the ranking system and your marketing strategy is to make Google see that you are, in fact, the best solution to the problem being searched.

Despite the obvious importance of reviews, many law firms are simply not getting reviews. As a general rule, law firms get fewer reviews because many clients are hesitant to talk about their legal problems online in a public forum. Understandably, some people don't want to let others know about their DUI or divorce. Moreover, leaving a review for a restaurant or a book is an ingrained habit, more so than leaving a review for your estate planning attorney.

We've done extensive research specifically with attorneys, and hardly any of them receive reviews, as evidenced by this Google+ Local page:

See *Figure* 17 .

Figure 17: Law firms typically do not have many reviews on Google.

Most of the law firms on this page have a Google+ Local page but no reviews attached to them at all. Only one firm has a review, and, in this case, it is only one review—not enough for the stars to even show up. This does not have to happen to your firm. You can see that you don't need to get a mountain of reviews on your directory listings and Google+ Local page to triumph over your competitors.

To start, you have to determine how many reviews you need to rank. Do some research to find out how many reviews your competitors have. Search for your keywords on Google, and see how many reviews the top-ranked results have. If they have five reviews, you need 10, and if they have 200, well...you've got a lot of work to do. Typically, however, active law firms have somewhere between 10 and 20 reviews (though most markets don't have anyone with more than five reviews). In order to beat your competitors at the rankings game, you'll need to have about double the amount of reviews they have.

Keep in mind that these are total reviews: for example, if you need 20 reviews, you can get them over four months. That's just five reviews per month, which is certainly possible. We'll talk about how to get those reviews shortly.

Review Sites

Which sites should you focus on when getting reviews? There are tons of them out there. Some of them don't matter, and some of them do. How do you figure out which ones are worth your time and effort?

To start off, focus on Yelp, Avvo, and Google. Once you have at least five reviews for each of these sites then you can start looking to diversify your reviews.

BIG TIP

If you want to make getting reviews a little easier, start by asking people to leave you a paper review before they leave the office. If the reviewer has a Gmail account, send that person an email with the link to your Google+ page requesting that he or she leave that review on Google. If the reviewer does not have a Gmail account, send him or her to Avvo or Yelp.

Thankfully, there's a fairly efficient way to find other places to focus your efforts. Half of the work is already done for you; many of these review sites are also directory listing websites, and you've already listed yourself on the top directories. What you have to do, then, is a Google keyword search in your location and go through the search results.

You likely won't need to go digging down through the search result pages. You're just interested in the top five directories. In search results, look for the first three to five listings that refer to an online directory site, like Yelp, Citysearch, or SuperPages.

It's also okay if you don't initially find five sites; you may only find two or three in the beginning. This is normal; sometimes it can take search engines quite some time to properly index all of the information on the web. To give you some perspective, there are about 10 thousand new websites created every day. This is a gigantic amount of information for search engines to index, so there is often a lag time as the search engines crawl the pages and index them. Your mission here is to find the review sites that are ranked, and of those, find the top-ranked ones—these are the ones where you're going to focus your review techniques.

Getting Reviews

Now that you've narrowed down your target directories, it's time to get reviews on them. Start with your current clients: it will be easier to get reviews from them because they're currently working with you.

 BIG TIP

If there are a large number of reviews on your competitors' listings in your keyword niche, consider focusing your efforts on one or two directory sites. This isn't something you will likely have to deal with, as the attorney market isn't normally saturated with reviews. If you do have a competitor with a high number of reviews, however, search for the firm's keywords on Google to see which review sites are consistently coming up. Then, focus all of your efforts on those sites. As an example, if your keyword is "VA benefits San Francisco, California" and the majority of reviews are being pulled from Citysearch and Avvo, then Citysearch and Avvo are the best places to start.

It's important to note that we understand that some attorneys are not allowed to ask for testimonials, depending on the state. However, you should know that you are not asking for a testimonial; you are simply asking someone to go to a website and leave a review. Review sites are a public forum, and clients can leave the review there with or without your assistance. That being said, there are some ethical issues that can arise when requesting reviews, so you do need to be careful.

THE ETHICS OF ONLINE REVIEWS

From Florida to Ohio, several states' ethics boards are beginning to adopt a stance that will have a major impact on how attorneys increase the amount of online reviews for their firms. What is the issue? Recently, several states have begun holding attorneys responsible for the content of reviews when the attorney requested the reviews.

It is common practice for law firms to reach out to clients and ask them to leave reviews on websites like Google and Yelp. In fact, we encourage this practice. Reviews are enormously beneficial for both your online ranking and your conversions. Having as few as five reviews and an overall rating of 4.5 stars on Google does have an impact on a new prospect's decision to potentially hire your firm.

We must point out two important clarifications to the ethics rulings:

1.   You are *not* responsible for the content of reviews that you did not request.

2.   You can still ask people to leave you a review.

But what happens if a review goes wrong? Let's say that a client goes to your Google+ Local page and leaves you the following review:

> "If you have been in an accident, you MUST call John. He is the best attorney in all of Miami. He won me

over $1 million in a settlement with AMC insurance company...and we settled out of court! If you are looking to win, there is no question that John will get you the money you deserve!"

There are clearly many ethical violations in the above review. If this review were a testimonial, you would not be able to put this on your website or use it in any other advertising medium. (Even though reviews are not technically advertising, they are treated similarly.)

The other issue here is that most review sites will not take down a review just because it violates your governing body's ethical guidelines. If it is within the review website's terms of service, you are out of luck. So, how do you ask for reviews while making sure that you do not violate any ethics rules?

When asking for reviews, make sure that you let the client know what they cannot say. It is perfectly acceptable to set parameters for the client. Include something along these lines: "We would be grateful if you would take a moment to leave us a review on Google+ Local. Please remember to avoid discussing any details of your case, and do not make any promises about our firm's services. If you will, just let people know if you enjoyed the experience of working with our firm. We greatly appreciate your time."

In the event that a client goes rogue and posts whatever he or she wants, do not panic. Send an email thanking him or her for the review, and ask that he or she either edit or remove the review, as it violates your state's ethical guidelines.

We used to encourage attorneys to hand out cards and email their clients, asking them to leave a review. We still recommend this strategy, but feel that you now need to tread carefully based on the ethical issues discussed earlier.

You cannot, under any circumstances, go to a website and create reviews for your own law firm. Falsifying reviews is illegal. Your clients also cannot give you the reviews on paper and have you write the reviews for them from your computer. This rule also extends to other computers in your office. It is common for firms to have a "review" computer set up in the office where clients can write a review. We always warn clients against these review-gathering strategies.

Why can't you write reviews for your clients or have a review computer in your office? Google tracks the location where the review was given. If your reviews all come from one IP address (the address of your computer and your office Wi-Fi), the reviews will look fake. It is common for scammers to have teams of people write multiple false reviews, and because of this, Google and other online review sites (like Yelp) actively search for and penalize these fake reviews.

Unfortunately, Google can't distinguish between fake reviews written by scammers and legitimate reviews all typed in your office. Therefore, under no circumstances should your clients write reviews from a network at your location. Instead, they should use their smartphone or tablet (given the devices are not using your Wi-Fi network) while in your office, or write the review somewhere else. This is very important: if you don't do this, your reviews will do nothing for your ranking.

Be extremely careful when hiring someone to help you with your review process. Many services will claim to be able to get you lots of reviews. The only thing an agency can do is help guide you on the process. If they play any role in the actual acquiring of reviews, you are opening yourself up for serious ethics violations. Often these "services" will create all of the reviews themselves and post them from one IP address. Google and other review sites can tell that the reviews written by these services are fake. As a result, the reviews will not benefit your online presence. In addition, this sort of review fabrication is against the law.

This past year, Google, Yelp, and even an attorney general increasingly targeted companies faking reviews. Google filtered a number of reviews from Google+ Local pages with no explanation. Yelp sued a law firm for repeatedly trying to create fake reviews on its Yelp listing. And, in September 2013, the attorney general of New York executed a sting operation investigating businesses using fake reviews and issued penalties totaling $350,000.

We do not recommend that you use a service at all. If you absolutely must, make sure that you build your process with a proven agency or partner. We provide our clients with a complete review process and require them to ask for reviews from their real clients for the reasons outlined earlier.

Ultimately, you and your firm are responsible for what is published in your name. If you hire a company to provide reviews and it cheats the system, you are held liable by both the online community and your bar association.

Bottom line? Do not create or purchase fake reviews. Ever.

See *Figure 18*.

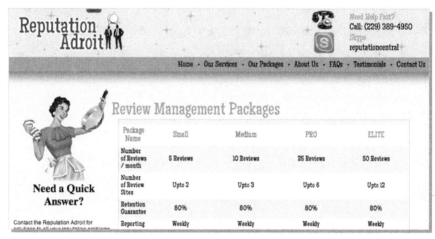

Figure 18: Example of a review service. Avoid these services.

The best way to get reviews, as already mentioned, is to hand out your card. Don't stop there, however. You can also mail or email clients to ask for reviews. Of course, keep in mind the ethical issues we discussed. See *Figure 19*.

Dear Client,

Thank you for working with our law firm. To help others just like you find our firm and know the work we do it would be appreciated if you could take five minutes to leave us a review online.

Please avoid using words like "best" or "guarantee." Just say what it was like to work with our firm.

Here are links to our profiles:
http://AVVO.com/attorneyprofile
http://Yelp.com/attorneyprofile
http://Google.Plus.com/firmprofile

Thank you in advance for your time.

Sincerely,
Lawyer

Figure 19: Sample template for requesting reviews

Note that this isn't all about Google+ Local; you want to send people to a few different directories. You do, of course, want reviews on Google+ Local, but you also need to diversify. Request reviews on other sites as well, such as Yelp, Avvo, Citysearch, and the others that you've identified as your target directory listings. (Try not to put your requests for each review site all on one card. It looks cramped, awkward, and unprofessional. A card per review site looks much more professional and will work better in getting clients to go to the review sites for you.)

Your clients may already have an account on one of these sites, and it would be easy for them to leave a review saying what a wonderful job you did. Look at your client's email address. If it ends in "gmail.com," send them the Google+ card, and if it ends in "yahoo.com," send them the Yahoo! Local card. This helps your ranking even more, as identified reviews are given more weight than anonymous ones.

Again, it's important to note that reviews are absolutely, positively, *not* testimonials; these are reviews that consumers can do on their own. In fact, you're only trying to encourage a behavior that's already happening. Don't be surprised if, when you start this process, you find that you already have a couple of reviews scattered around the Internet. When you ask, you'll find that, more often than not, people are more than willing to help you by writing reviews.

Reviews are one of the driving forces behind Google+ Local rankings. By having this process for reviews, you're ensuring your steady climb to the top.

Avvo

Avvo is a unique review site in that it separates reviews from clients and endorsements from peer attorneys. Avvo takes many things into account when determining your rating, including peer reviews, but not client reviews. We recommend that you ask a few of your peers to leave an endorsement for you on Avvo. You shouldn't have to tell them to avoid violating ethical guidelines in your state, but it doesn't hurt to remind them anyway. Having a strong Avvo rating is beneficial not only because it shows up in search results but also because you can put the Avvo badge on your website, which can increase your credibility.

Reputation Defense: A Good Offense Is the Best Defense

When covering your web presence and online reviews, we would be remiss if we didn't include negative reviews. What happens when you get negative reviews?

As a lawyer, your professional reputation is a critical part of your overall success and career. Unfortunately, the truth about the Internet is that anyone, anonymously, can post anything they want to about you. Blog posts, online reviews, websites, social media—there is no end to the opportunities that people have to talk about you. In some cases, this is a positive thing, as we have discussed so far. In others, this can be extremely damaging, causing you to lose clients.

To manage your reputation online, you have to be aware of what is currently posted about you, your firm, and your partners. How do you do this? On Google, you can search for phrases in quotation marks and get returns that must include every word in the phrase. For example, you can type your name in quotation marks in the search box, and Google will show you every website with your name on it. This can be difficult if you have a common name. If this is the case for you, try typing in your name with and without your middle initial. After you search with your name only, add the word "attorney" or "scam" following your search phrase (e.g., "Joe Smith attorney" or "Joe Smith scam"). When searching, go through the first 30 pages or so of Google and look for anything about you. Click on each page with a mention of your name, and read what it says.

The next thing you should do is set up a Google Alert. Google Alert is a service that acts as an alert, emailing you any information you have requested that shows up in search. It is not 100 percent accurate all the time, but it is fairly reliable. If you add your name in quotation marks to Google Alert, Google will email you the websites that mention you every time your name appears online. You should set up a Google Alert for not only your name but also your firm name and the names of the firm's partners. This is a great tool for monitoring your reputation, as it keeps you up to speed on who is talking about you. If someone leaves a negative review about you online, you will be notified of the review and will be able to take appropriate action.

As you monitor your online reputation, remember that very few people visit the second page of Google, let alone the third or fourth. If you find something negative about you or your firm on the ninth page of Google, you may want to just leave it alone; no one is going to find it anyway. Acting on something that is buried deep in search results can cause it to rise in the rankings, which is something you want to avoid at all costs. But if the negative item is high enough in the search results, you need to act.

What do you do if you find something about you that is totally false and damaging to your reputation?

You are an attorney; send the commenter a strongly worded letter telling him or her to take the information down. If contact information is not readily available, you may be able to find it by entering the website URL in the whois. net search (http://who.is). Of course, do not threaten them, but be firm and brief. Usually, just asking someone to pull the content down is enough. Depending on the specifics of your situation, you may need to take further action.

What do you do if you find something about you that is true and damaging to your reputation?

Make no mistake: this is going to happen. No matter how great your service, you will not be able to make every client absolutely happy. Some clients are going to be angry about how things ended up, and they will express their unhappiness and frustration online. You need to be prepared for this.

When you find negative and disparaging remarks, remain calm. It is difficult not to take this sort of thing personally, but you need to act with a cool head. First, you should see if you are in a place to respond to the comment. Some websites will allow you to comment, and some situations will warrant a reply. When replying, do not get angry or defensive—this will only make the situation worse. Remember that your response will be visible not only to the person who made the negative comment but also to many of your prospects. Think about your reply carefully, and craft it as if a new prospect were reading both the complaint and your response. Do you come across as suspect in your reply? If so, rewrite it. It may also be beneficial for you to have someone else read your reply before you submit it. Keep in mind that you are writing the response to help a prospective client understand the situation, not to disagree or argue with the original reviewer. Also, be wary of violating any ethical guidelines when replying. The most common mistake is providing details to the situation that are not public information; please avoid using details, and keep it super short.

If you can, it is occasionally helpful to contact the person who posted and talk to him or her about the issue. You can always politely ask that person to take down the comment. If you make an effort to remedy the situation, some clients will be satisfied and will remove the negative remarks.

If the complaint is truly justified, consider this a learning moment. Take a hard look at your practice, and make the appropriate adjustments to better your service. This takes more courage than just sweeping the complaint under the rug. Truly great attorneys know when they could've done something better and will make the right changes to avoid future mistakes. Be one of those attorneys.

Managing Negative Remarks That Are Ranking High in Search

Because you now know that few people navigate to Page 2 and beyond of search results, you can use this to your advantage. If you can't remove or respond to negative content, your goal should be to push it so far down in search results that the average person will never find it.

How do you do this? You work to have other websites that you *can* control rank above the website with the negative content. Your targeted goal should be about 19 unique websites. Here is a list of the best places to start (a lot of these websites will rank highly with minimal effort):

1) Your own website
2) Google+
3) Facebook
4) LinkedIn
5) Twitter
6) Thumbtack
7) Avvo
8) About.me
9) Yelp
10) MerchantCircle
11) Amazon
12) Pinterest
13) Better Business Bureau

14) Chamber of commerce

15) Local bar association

16) National bar association

17) Press releases

18) Blogs

19) Videos

By creating complete and active accounts on all of these platforms, you can help to ensure that any negative information will be pushed to deeper pages; this is usually more than enough to solve any issue. When the issue involves comments that are far too harsh, such as when a furious client calls you a scam artist, you should include some posts on the above sites that talk about "scams" or "rip-offs" to help those sites outrank the negative comments.

Managing Negative Reviews

Just like negative remarks, negative reviews are inevitable. Some clients will have complaints that are justified; others will simply be impossible to please, no matter what you do. When you find a negative review on Google+ Local or another review site, you can respond in much the same way that you do to a negative remark: you can write a carefully worded reply or contact the client to remove the review. In addition, you can respond by increasing your efforts to get positive reviews. If you get a negative review, immediately reach out to a few happy clients, and ask them personally to review your firm at the same website that features the negative review.

Fortunately, having a few negative reviews on directory sites can actually be a good thing. If this sounds counterintuitive, take a moment to think about human behavior; have you ever heard of the phrase "too good to be true"? If prospects think that your reviews appear too positive, they may wonder if the reviews are fake. Having a good mix of reviews—mostly positive with a few negative—will make your firm look more credible to prospects. Moreover, if one out of every 10 reviews is negative, people will be very forgiving: we all know that one person who is never satisfied and complains too much.

- Reviews can and do influence Google's (and other search engines') ranking system. Reviews provide credibility to your firm and give search engines an indication of your firm's worthiness to be ranked highly.

- As an attorney, you will need about twice as many reviews as the competitors in your keyword niche. Most attorneys, unless they are in a very competitive area, need only around 10 to 20 reviews.

- Because most review sites are also directory sites, you only need to search the top directory sites for your keywords and get reviews there. You should get reviews on several different sites, one of which *must* be your Google+ Local page.

- Be mindful of your state's ethical guidelines when asking for reviews. In some states, ethics boards have ruled that, as soon as you ask for a review, you are responsible for what the client posts online.

- Faking reviews is illegal. Also, fake reviews will not fool Google; you will be ignored or even penalized in the rankings for having fake reviews.

- You should not have a computer in your office for clients to leave reviews. Because the reviews will come from one IP address, Google will think that they are spam and will therefore ignore them.

- Beware of companies that offer to get your firm reviews fast. Many services that promise a large amount of reviews in a short amount of time are scammers that write fake reviews— which are illegal and ineffective. You will be held responsible for what they write in your name.

- Reviews are *not* testimonials. By asking for reviews, you are simply encouraging a behavior that people already do. To request reviews, hand out cards to your clients with the link to your listings.

- As an attorney, your professional reputation is extremely important to your career, which means that you must manage your online reputation.

- To manage your online reputation, you need to know what is being said about you online. To find out, do several searches for your name in quotation marks, followed by searches for your name with the words "attorney," "scam," "rip-off," etc.

- If you find a negative comment that is false and damaging, you may want to ask the commenter to take it down. If you find a negative comment that is substantiated, you may want to calmly reply in order to fix the situation.

- If you find negative reviews that rank highly in search results, don't worry: all is not lost! Aim to have around 20 websites featuring positive content that you control rank for your name and firm name. Start with your own website, Facebook, Avvo, Yelp, etc. These websites should bury the negative reviews where no one will find them in search results.

- Remember that few people visit the second page of Google, and next to no one visits the pages after that.

- A mix of good and bad reviews can be a good thing! While you want mostly good reviews, a bad review or two can assure skeptical people that your good reviews are honest and not a scam.

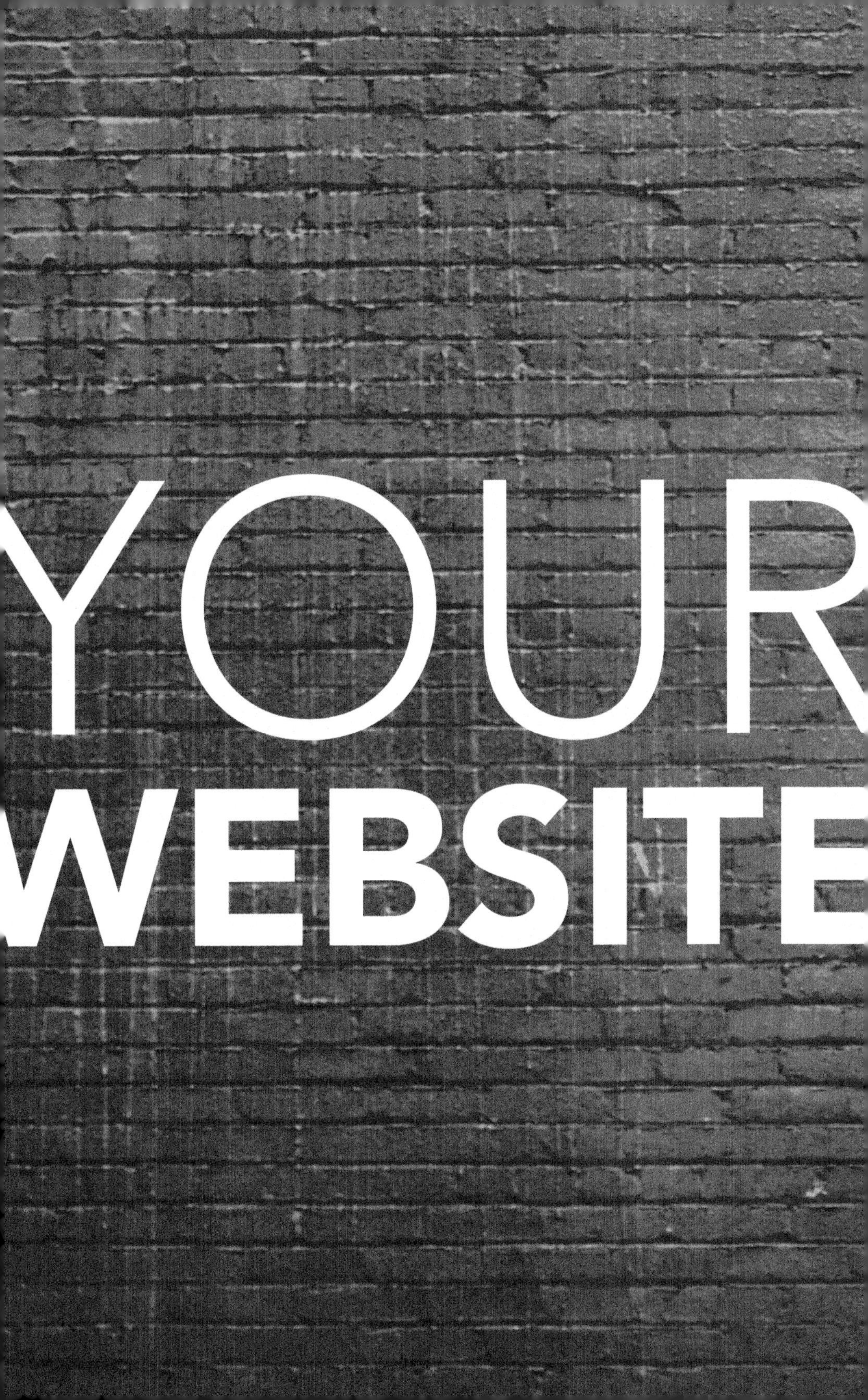
YOUR
WEBSITE

SECTION 2:
YOUR WEBSITE

LEGAL WEBSITES

COMMUNICATE
SOLVE
INFORM
SERVE

MARKETING

COMMUNICATE
SOLVE
INFORM
SERVE

SOLVE
INFORM
SERVE

PAST

PRESENT

2002

2015

MOBILE WEBSITES PAGE 171

29%

OF ALL TRAFFIC
TO LEGAL SITES
IS FROM A
MOBILE DEVICE

**MORE USERS
ACCESSED THE
INTERNET**

FROM
MOBILE
DEVICES

**THAN DESKTOPS
IN 2014**

LOAD
TIME

**SHOULD BE
LESS THAN**

< 1 SEC

BLOGGING

WRITE FOR CONSUMERS

NOT LAWYERS

TALK ABOUT

LOCAL EVENTS

COMMON LEGAL QUESTIONS

WHAT OTHER PEOPLE SAY

USE IMAGES

LEGAL 3 : 1 LOCAL

MEASURING YOUR ROI

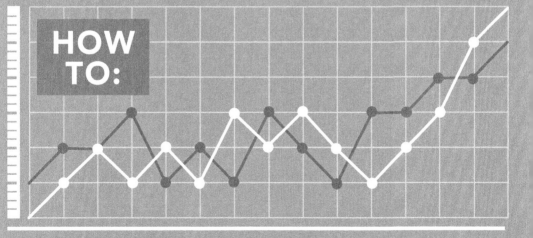

HOW TO:

TRACK   TEST   CALCULATE
RETURN ON INVESTMENT

Chapter 5:

Creating the Right Law Firm Website

See *Figure 20*. An important set of questions to ask yourself is when, why, and how people are deciding to visit your website.

To gain clarity on this topic, GNGF decided to run an independent consumer survey. Working with SurveyGizmo, we polled a broad cross section of people from coast to coast with less than 1 percent of participants coming from any particular city. Based on all total U.S. households, our survey had a +/- 5 percent margin of error.

Our first question was aimed at determining what people do when faced with a legal problem. Obviously, people take more than one action, so we allowed the survey participant to select all that applied.

According to our survey, where did people who were faced with a legal problem go?

Over 60 percent of participants said they would visit the Internet when faced with a legal problem. Shockingly, only 26 percent of the group said they would talk with a friend or family member.

This is not a sign that referrals are dead. It would be reasonable to assume that, when faced with a legal issue, people are turning to the Internet first to educate themselves before seeking a referral. This should come as great news for you because it means that, with the right web presence established, your law firm can be there to provide answers to future prospects.

This became further evident in the next question on the survey: "If you or someone you know needed to hire an attorney, how would you find an attorney?"

In this case, 51 percent said online and 67 percent said through a referral. (Again, since this is a "select all that apply" question, the responses will add up to more than 100 percent.) This falls in line with what we observe when marketing a law firm. Potential clients are still seeking out family and friends for a referral to an attorney. Yet, even after asking for a referral, lots of people are going to the Internet to research the law firm to which they were referred.

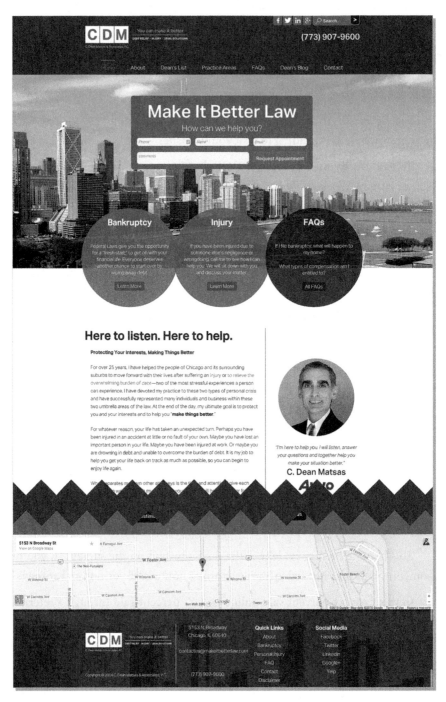

Figure 20: Example of a law firm's website homepage

This became very clear when we asked people when they were most likely to visit a law firm website. Only 9 percent of the participants said "never."

A majority (almost 64 percent) of respondents visit the law firm website before ever calling. A big surprise came, however, when almost 82 percent of those surveyed said they visit a law firm website (some even after they have contacted the firm) before they visit the office. That is about one in five people.

Lastly, we were curious if people would watch a video posted by a law firm about a legal topic relating to their situation. Over a third said they were likely or very likely, and less than 4 percent of the entire audience said "never." This means over 96 percent of your clients, prospects, and visitors will watch a video pertaining to their legal problem. See *Figure 21*.

What conclusions can we draw from this study?

Combining the information from this study with the data we have captured across all our legal clients over the last four years, the picture becomes very clear.

You must have a current, optimized, and professional website because your prospects are interested in the content on your website—text and video. Even after they've been referred to you by a friend, people are likely to visit your website, often before they ever contact you. If you are not providing the information they need online, you are likely losing out on business that your reputation already earned.

The biggest issue is that when people don't call you, for any reason, you don't know the business that you are losing. It is very difficult to track people who get to your website, can't find the information they need, and thus never call. Sometimes a person just wanted to get a quick answer to a complex problem, and having a video helped that person get that answer while reinforcing the need to call you at the same time.

Your website has two primary functions: to get traffic and convert visitors. We want to make sure that your website succeeds at both of these roles. What we *don't* want is for you to get too much traffic to your website that doesn't convert.

These two roles broadly cover referral business, new courses of business for your law firm, current clients, and employee acquisition.

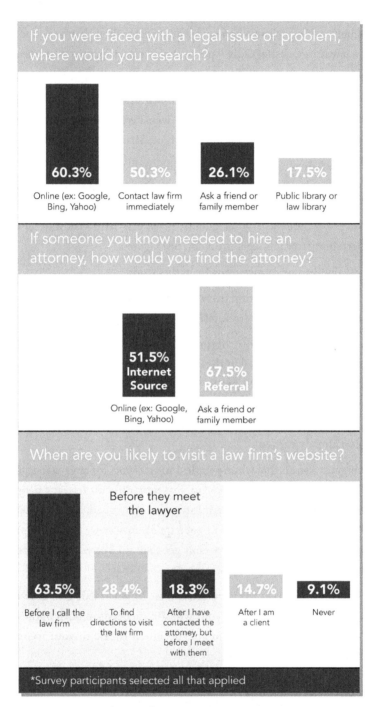

If you were faced with a legal issue or problem, where would you research?

60.3% Online (ex: Google, Bing, Yahoo)

50.3% Contact law firm immediately

26.1% Ask a friend or family member

17.5% Public library or law library

If someone you know needed to hire an attorney, how would you find the attorney?

51.5% Internet Source — Online (ex: Google, Bing, Yahoo)

67.5% Referral — Ask a friend or family member

When are you likely to visit a law firm's website?

Before they meet the lawyer

63.5% Before I call the law firm

28.4% To find directions to visit the law firm

18.3% After I have contacted the attorney, but before I meet with them

14.7% After I am a client

9.1% Never

*Survey participants selected all that applied

Figure 21: Example of a law firm's website homepage

We discussed brand earlier; that is your starting point for developing an effective website. Once you uncover your brand messaging, you are ready to plan your website flow, copy, images, blog content, etc.

Your website should have a blog. It does not matter what people say about the purpose of your blog. Your blog has to be within your website. We will talk more about what your blog is and how to blog later in this section, but first we need to address this pandemic problem in the legal industry.

When you create a good, thoughtful, purposeful blog that also happens to be part of your website, you are creating an authentic place for readers to engage with your content and learn the truth about your services. There is no reason to hide from your readers the fact that you have a law firm. Even if the only purpose of your blog is to establish expertise, you need not put that content on an island far away from your main brand. Embrace your firm's brand and image. Let your website become a platform for you to help the community and inform readers of the areas you practice.

Your online content does not stop there. If you have multiple practice areas, you should create unique sections of your website to address these practice areas. If you have multiple locations, then each location should get a stand-alone page on your website. You don't need a new website; all you need is a new interior page on your existing website. (We have seen some web agencies try to convince law firms to buy something new when all they need to do is add to what they already have. Don't fall for this shrewd trick.)

Creating a Website That Produces New Clients

Now, we know how important Google is, and we've taken a look at how recent changes have impacted local search returns and Google rankings, which are, in general, important to your marketing efforts. We know that traditional media is fading fast and when it does work well, often drives traffic online as much, if not more, than phone calls. If you want to stay on top of the game, you're going to have to get this online business straight—right away—because things are getting more competitive for every size firm. When we wrote our first edition of this book, there were far fewer law firms taking the steps to build their online presence correctly, if at all. Four years later, we have seen a huge movement in law firms getting online—and getting online right. That has led to significantly more competition online for all law firms, large and small.

You might think that the next step is to just get ranked, and that would be the wrong approach. The real goal of your website is to achieve both traffic (prospects visiting your site) and conversions (convincing prospects to contact you). If the goal were merely to rank, things would be simple. But over the last several years, we have seen the search returns from one user to the next become even more volatile. This does not mean that ranking is worthless, just that ranking is only a small piece of the larger pie and is ultimately impossible to accurately measure or report on. In fact, as mentioned earlier, all the Google changes have made it harder to know where you really rank; where someone is browsing from, what they have browsed before, whether they are browsing from a mobile device or a desktop—all these things influence what Google shows these potential clients. If you have a marketing agency that spends too much time reporting on ranking, be very concerned. That is not the key metric on which you should be judging the success of your Internet presence.

If you're going to get good conversions from your search rankings, you need a functional website that fully caters to both the needs of your firm and the needs of your clients.

Traffic is important, but a law firm website that has thousands of visitors and fails to convert them into real clients....is pointless.

The creation of a website can be a minefield, especially in today's whiz-bang world, where everyone thinks that every website needs interactive menus, drop-down interfaces, rotating pictures, and all sorts of other bells and whistles. You see it all the time, in fact: people ask for interactive websites, or developers try to push moving this or that, saying how important it is and how professional it makes a site look. And you may be tempted to believe them.

The truth is that all of this fancy stuff on a website may actually hurt your ability to convert people into new clients. This is important. A solid, simple website will work far better at getting clients to contact you. This may seem counter-intuitive, especially in a world that seems to value style over substance, but it's true. Simpler websites have been far more effective at conversion than flashier, more extravagant pages.

This does not mean that a law firm should sacrifice design. Please do not confuse "less fancy" with "poor design." You should still have a website that represents your firm well. The design should be professional, clean, and functional. Philosopher and mathematician Blaise Pascal once wrote, "I have made this longer than usual because I have not had time to make it shorter." Think about your website design in the same way. Take the time to think about the core visual and informational elements of your website and cut or move anything that doesn't have to be on the page. Having less flash on a website leads to better visual design because there is less clutter. And a better visual design helps with conversions. Creating a fancy website that has way too many functions is easy, but creating a simple website that maximizes your conversions takes time and energy.

Your website is an integral part of your online presence. Though it is by no means the most important link in the chain, your website needs to be done well. If done poorly, it has the potential to ruin your online efforts. The bottom line is this: if your referrals or prospects don't actually pick up the phone and call, all of the effort that you put into your website has been wasted. No matter how flashy, how fancy, how up-to-date your website is, if there are no conversions, your website is simply not working for you.

What Does a "Good" Website Look Like?

Often, lawyers ask us what the secret is to getting visitors to pick up the phone and call. Before we jump into those details, there is a very important topic we must discuss: cheap-looking websites.

In today's market, the data shows that having a website is an expectation by your current and future clients. The website you have is a direct reflection of your firm. As we mentioned earlier, the recent study that we commissioned in the summer of 2014 found that only 9.5 percent of Americans claimed to have never visited a law firm website. Over 90 percent of Americans in the study—people just like your clients—said they visited a law firm's website either before they called or before visiting the office after booking an appointment.

BIG TIP

Law firms are losing referral business every month because their website and web presence is not current. We are seeing firms that have a poor website design losing more referral business than ever before. Times have changed for referral business. Have you ever spoken with someone at a networking event or been told by clients that they would give your firm's name out as a referral, only to suddenly watch those prospects vanish? If so, it was likely due to a poorly designed website.

You are losing potential clients you didn't even know you had.

In your firm's office, you would not have a dead plant, broken chairs, and a dirty waiting room. Your office should be professional, presentable, and attractive. Well, guess what? Your website needs to be as professional as your office. People searching for a lawyer hold you to a higher standard than the local dry cleaner. Having a website that looks like it was designed circa 2008 by your cousin's nephew-in-law in his parent's basement is damaging to your professional image and flat out makes you look bad.

Take a look at your website and a few of your local competitors. How do you compare? Now think about the fact that your website may be the first impression you make. Are you proud of your website, and do you believe that your prospect will look at it with a feeling of excitement to call your office?

What constitutes a well-designed site that actually converts traffic into prospects? There are a few things. Let's take a look at them and find out how to build the website that will get the most visitors to call your office.

Site Construction: What Should Your Overall Site Look Like?

In general, there is a rule that can be applied to websites looking to garner conversions. We've mentioned that the less fancy the website is, the more conversions you'll get from it. Solid, functional sites will be far more effective. With that mentality in mind, here is a general outline of what a simple website layout might look like:

Navigation:

1) Homepage

2) About the Attorney pages

3) Practice Areas page

4) Blog

5) Contact Us page (with map and phone number)

And that is all you need. There is room to add a little more, but avoid going overboard.

It might seem a bit *underwhelming* to you—not to mention vastly smaller than the majority of the websites you've visited—and you're right. Those websites, however, are not ours. Your website should be lean and mean, built for one purpose and one purpose only: to get people who go to your website to call you or email you. Anything else is a waste. It's nice that people come to visit your site, but that doesn't mean anything for your business if no one calls or if you don't capture someone's phone or email for future follow-up. The goal is to make a website that is not cumbersome or difficult to navigate. If it is, this will cause people to get frustrated and leave your site. It is too easy for potential clients to just hit the back button and go to the next person on the Google search, if they are even the tiniest bit confused or frustrated by a website.

This is, of course, just an example. You are free to modify this layout however you wish. Depending on your firm, you may want to add a page about upcoming events you are hosting or recent news about your firm. Just know that this basic layout works extremely well, and always, always remember this: the less complex, the better the results.

When people visit your website, you have a limited time to connect with them before they move on to another site. We call this the 2-20-2-20 rule. You have less than two seconds to earn a prospect's next 20 seconds. In those 20 seconds, the visitor will determine if you earn his or her next two minutes. After those two minutes, the prospect will decide if he or she will call or email your firm and give you another 20 minutes to convince that prospect that you are the right lawyer to solve his or her legal issue.

A simple, easy layout keeps a user's eyes on your website for more than 2 seconds. Having a cluttered, busy website with too many options or moving graphics decreases your chances of getting to the next 20 seconds.

Your firm may have already worked with a marketing agency to create a logo and set of colors that represent your brand. If so, implement those into your website design. (Your website should act as an extension of your offline brand: your marketing efforts, whether online or off, should be cohesive and integrated.) Having colors that clash or don't match your brand can cause someone to leave your website. There are a number of color palette tools available online that allow you to enter your firm's core colors. They will suggest visually appealing, complementary colors. For example, try Colour Lovers (**http://www.colourlovers.com**) or Color Combos (**http://www.colorcombos.com**).

Homepage: Your First Impression

Your homepage serves only a few functions: validate to a referral that you are a great choice, give all users a strong sense of your brand, and help new users navigate to important information. With well-written copy, good images, video, and proper conversion elements, your homepage will act as a portal to move people in the right direction. All of these elements will cognitively engage prospects and lead to you earning his or her next 20 seconds.

THE DEATH OF ROTATING IMAGES:

Tim Ash, author of Landing Page Optimization, among other researchers, discovered in testing that if there is movement on the page while the user is engaging with the website, the reptilian portion of the brain is activated. (This is the part responsible for the fight-or-flight response.) What happens? Every time there is movement on the page, the user's mind prevents the user from engaging with your content and forces him or her to assess the situation. Basically, the user is determining whether or not the movement is something he or she needs to worry about. The best example of this would be when you are reading a book and, out of the corner of your eye, you see a bug start crawling next to you. Even though the bug is likely no real threat, your mind will stop you from reading and divert your attention to the movement. When this happens to a visitor of your website, it dramatically increases the odds that the person will leave your website without taking action. You've lost that prospect.

In addition to being easy on the eyes and free of distracting movement, your website's homepage should have several key components. It should feature images of lawyers at your firm, your blog, a video, and compelling copy.

You may have noticed that many law firm websites are littered with practically identical stock photos—legal books, gavels, scales of justice, etc. This is a great area to differentiate yourself and help the website visitor get to know you better. Prospects like to get to know the person they are about to call and possibly hire, and our data shows they click on the pictures of lawyers (expecting to be taken to the About the Attorney pages) on the homepage more than anything else. We highly encourage you to take some quality photos of people in your firm in the setting of your office. Taking the time to have a professional photographer take some quality photos of your staff and office will help increase conversions from your web presence.

Furthermore, incorporating a small, short (60 to 90 seconds long) video somewhere on your homepage will boost your conversions by about 100 percent. GNGF conducted a case study comparing websites with video, websites without video, and websites that had video on the homepage. The end results were astounding. It turns out that users don't even have to watch the video for it to have an impact. Just having a video is enough to create more conversion, and more conversion means more business for your firm.

We like to feature this video on the right-hand side of the homepage. Have your web team add a light box to the video. This will allow the video to pop out of the side to the middle of the page. The coding on this is minimal and shouldn't be an issue for any competent Webmaster.

For this short homepage video, we recommend explaining why you practice the type of law you do, what you like about your community, and what prospects can expect when working with your firm.

Homepage Copy

Of course, you will also need to have copy on your homepage. For many attorneys, their homepage reads like a biography of their greatest accomplishments. Does the following sound familiar?

> Smith, Johnson & Doe Law Firm LLC was founded in 19?? in [City], [State]. Smith graduated from [very prominent law school] in 19??, following three years of service at [organization], where he received many accolades. Johnson graduated summa cum laude from [another very prominent law school], and after spending two years as a clerk under [very impressive judge], he won [this amazing award]. Doe? Well, Doe is just incredible.

You get the idea. While you should certainly be proud of your accomplishments, the homepage is simply the wrong place to put this information.

Instead, your homepage should have what is called "consumer advocacy copy." This is crucial: when people search for the services that you provide, they are trying to solve a problem. This could be a divorce, death of a loved one, or contract negotiation. The essential thing to remember is that they have a problem that needs to be solved, and your website should speak to the solutions they are after.

The copy on your homepage should include no more than three things:

1) The benefits that your firm provides your clients. (Not your services, but the actual benefits that clients receive as a result of working with you.)

2) Information about topics on your blog, as well as links and enticements to the good content on your website.

3) Calls to action and a place that the users can request further contact via email.

These three items are so important to the success of a website that, for our clients, we write these sections on their behalf and place them word-for-word on the homepage.

Typically, a well-written homepage will start something like this:

Here at Smith, Johnson & Doe, we pride ourselves on helping our clients navigate the confusing terrain of divorce. We understand this can be a confusing and difficult time for you and your family. Our attorneys take the time to get to know your unique situation and help you understand the options you have to solve your problem.

Hopefully, you get the idea. The point is to speak directly to the emotions that your prospects are feeling while visiting your website. If they are seeking a divorce, their emotional state may be characterized by frustration, fear, and angst. Someone starting a new company, on the other hand, is likely excited and looking to get moving. Use as many emotional words as you can; this will help your prospects feel connected to your firm. When people feel that you understand them emotionally, they will be more likely to convert into a real client.

People purchase based on emotion and then justify their purchase with logic. This is precisely why you should move your accolades to the profile page on your website. Use the first place that people connect with your website (your homepage) as a place to give them emotional assurance that you understand their needs, and let them move to the logical, research part of the sales cycle on their own.

Your homepage copy should also have links to other areas within your website, or "cross-links." These links connect the user to more in-depth information about specific topics while they are reading. If you talk about car accidents on your homepage, you should link from there to an interior page about car accident information. The same goes for all practice areas that you reference on your homepage.

Cross-linking on your homepage and throughout your website is not only helpful for your visitors but also beneficial for your rankings. This is mostly caused by an increase in the user's interaction with your website, which indicates to search engines that your website is providing the right answer for the person's search query.

See *Figures 22 & 23.*

About the Attorneys Pages

The "About the Attorney" pages are, oddly enough, ones that many firms get wrong. These are typically the second most frequently visited pages on the website. For this reason, it is odd that law firms are not paying special attention to these pages. Often, attorneys are content to just throw in a short paragraph about themselves or the partners and perhaps a map with directions for how to get to the firm. This isn't enough information about your firm, nor is it helping you drive conversions.

Yes, people care about your years of experience as a lawyer. But that's not what's going to get them to call. The number of years you've been in practice doesn't truly distinguish you from the other lawyers in the area, and it doesn't give prospects a reason to give you their business.

Like your homepage, you need to speak to how working with your firm will benefit your prospects. Think about it this way. Most people care about one thing and one thing only: WIIFM. That stands for "What's In It For Me?". Honestly, your prospects couldn't care less about your degrees, titles, or positions—sorry. What they really want to know is if you can solve their problem quickly and professionally. So, instead of talking about you, talk about them and why they will benefit from working with you. In fact, this alone will set your website above and beyond most of the law firm sites we see: they simply

Figure 22: Example of a law firm's website homepage

Figure 23: Example of a law firm's website homepage

don't set themselves apart sufficiently, and in doing so, you'll gain a very competitive edge in this field.

In addition to your "About the Attorney" pages, you can add a page about the firm as a whole. Just like your homepage, make sure the content talks about how your firm can help the prospective client and what sets your firm apart from the others.

See *Figure 24* & *Figure 25*.

Figure 24: Example of an "About the Attorney" website page

The
Farrish Law Firm LPA

Search   513-403-9699

MEET WITH AN ATTORNEY

Name

Phone

Email

SEND US A MESSAGE

Comments

Kelly Farrish

Learn About Managing Partner, Kelly Farrish

Kelly Farrish always knew he wanted to be an attorney, but he the path he took to get there isn't like most. He served five years in the United States Air Force and did two voluntary years in South Vietnam. When he returned to Cincinnati, he worked the midnight shift as a technician at Cincinnati Bell, all the while attending college full time year round for three years. He graduated Cum Laude from the University of Cincinnati. Upon promotion to the marketing department, Kelly then continued to work full time at Cincinnati Bell while attending Chase Law School year round at night for four years.

He's now practiced DUI law for 36 years. He is also a frequent speaker on DUI for the Cincinnati Bar Association and the annual statewide Ohio State Bar Association DUI Seminar. Not only that, but he has been a speaker at many DUI seminars and speaks to private groups and organizations upon request. He also taught at the University of Cincinnati in the undergraduate program for about 10 years.

If you asked Kelly Farrish what his favorite part of being an attorney is, he'd tell you that it is really being able to help people who have run into difficulties. Kelly also thoroughly enjoys being in the courtroom and fighting for an individual's rights in court. Ultimately, he wants to substantially reduce the initial stress that his clients are under and provide assistance that has long-term benefits, and sometimes even lifetime benefits.

One of Kelly's proudest moments was serving as the general contractor through the total renovation of 810 Sycamore Street, a building that provides office sharing space for 110 attorneys. Kelly served as the general contractor; he designed it, furnished the building, and now manages it.

When Kelly's not in the office or at court, he enjoys doing things for veterans involved with the Veterans Court in the Hamilton County Municipal Court, presenting seminars to the public about the DUI process and teaching. You may catch him at a Cincinnati sports game–he's a loyal fan; Go UC Bearcats, Cincinnati Reds, and Cincinnati Bengals! He loves to eat out and enjoy Cincinnati's restaurants, Silverglades Delicatessen, El Coyote in Anderson Township, Ruby's and Seasons 52 being his favorites.

When it comes to television Kelly sticks to sports–if you can't hit it, kick it, or bounce it he probably doesn't watch it. While he loves to watch the game, *Butch Cassidy and the Sundance Kid*, and *Patton*, are two of his all time favorite movies.

Read below to learn more about Kelly Farrish's education and prolific experience as a DUI attorney:

Areas of Practice

- DUI / DWI / OVI

Litigation Percentage

- 100% of Practice Devoted to Litigation

Certified Legal Specialties

- Qualified Instructor, National Highway Traffic Administration Field Sobriety Tests

Figure 25: Example of an "About the Attorney" website page

Practice Area Pages

These pages are straightforward. What are the various areas of law that you practice?

In the beginning, you should not attempt to add every practice area you are able to handle. Instead, focus on one or two areas first. By niching your practice areas, you are focusing your web efforts and more effectively communicating to the search engines what you do. There is the old cliché that "the jack of all trades is a master of none." Don't be a master of none.

Look at your web presence as dynamic as opposed to static: you should be consistently editing and adding to your website. If you are a bankruptcy law firm, for example, try adding a few types of bankruptcy law in the beginning and then, over time, adding the remaining areas. This adds valuable new content to your website on a regular basis, similar to what you do for your blog.

Your "Practice Areas" section should be broken down into a specific hierarchy. To continue with our previous bankruptcy law firm example, the website should have a main "Bankruptcy" page and several sub-pages on the various types of bankruptcy: Chapter 13, Chapter 11, Chapter 7, etc. If your prospects are on your homepage, allow them the option to navigate to the main practice area while also providing a drop-down menu of the various internal categories within the main area. Why should you do this? Think about the user's experience; organizing your website this way helps your prospects navigate your website.

See *Figure 26.*

Internal pages should have the following:

1) Images that show the reader what the page represents

2) At least two paragraphs of information explaining the practice area

3) The benefits of working with your firm

4) Links to other areas of your website, including other practice areas

We recommend the length of the page to be about 800–1,000 words. That is a lot of opportunity to spend time on the benefits of working with your firm, your experience in that practice area, and specifics about that practice area that can help your visitor understand a little more about whether or not this will

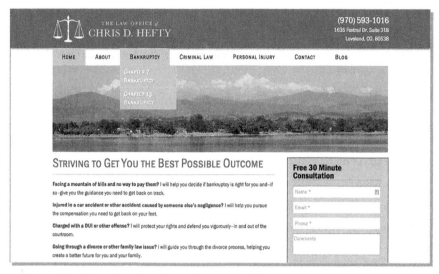

Figure 26: Example of a drop-down menu for practice areas

solve his or her problem. Remember, your visitor likely came to your website and visited your practice area page because he or she went to Google to solve a problem.

Keep the links on any given page to a minimum. Typically, you are allowed, without penalty from the search engines, up to 40 links on a page. For a law firm, the number of links should be between 15 and 30, but this includes links in your header and footer, too, so don't forget to count those.

After you add a main practice area page, add at least one new page to your practice areas every three months. You can add practice areas more often, but there are other new pages you should be adding over time as well.

Contact Page

The "Contact Us" page should be very simple. You should include your email, your phone number, and a Google map to your firm. You might also consider including written directions to your office from two places, or the similar Google Maps directions function. That's it. You can perhaps put a slightly different or stronger call to action on this page, but for the most part, this page should be clean and simple, with nothing to distract visitors from picking up the phone or putting in their email. Some firms add a contact form on this page. That is fine, but the most important thing is to provide a clear phone number or email that is directed and answered by an actual human.

See *Figure 27.*

Figure 27: Example of a law firm's "Contact Us" website page

Other Pages

There are numerous options with regard to the types of other pages you can add to your website. Here is a list of pages that fit well within the legal market:

City or Community Pages: Like most firms, you likely want to draw business from beyond a 10 mile radius of your office. The old method we have seen many marketers use to try to get a website to rank in other locations was to stuff the bottom of your website with every nearby city and county. This is not only *not* recommended, but it could potentially be flagged as spammy content by Google and be penalized. The best method for getting website traffic from your surrounding area is to use pages written about various practice areas that target locations outside your city. Try writing a few pages about a practice area and insert specific data about the city next door. Adding one of these pages a month will give you 12 more pages by the end of the year.

In the News Page: If you are in the news regularly, then add a page where you can link to the various times you were featured in the media. This would include videos from local news stations, podcasts from radio stations, articles you were mentioned in, and so on. Also, sometimes you have news that may not be in the media. For instance, maybe a lawyer at the firm was added to a local non-profit board, but there was no specific press mention. You can add your own article about it on your website (maybe in your blog, hint, hint) and put a link to it here.

Video Gallery Page: When you record your videos, you will have at least 10 to 20 content videos. Create a page where users can access all the videos at once after you have added the videos to your blog.

Testimonials Page: Depending on your state bar association's professional rules of conduct, you may not be able to add testimonials to your website. Please check with your bar before adding this type of page.

Call to Action

So, you've got the basic layout of your pages. Now, there is just one thing left: your call to action. Every page within your website should include this.

What makes an effective call to action, and how can you put that to use on your site to generate conversions? An effective call to action is one that makes customers pick up the phone and call or give you their email address right away. It is not one thing, one line, or one strategy: it is a strategy that continues throughout your entire website. It's crucial that your call to action be very strong because you're asking for information that has become more and more private.

There are three ways to create a strong call to action. We recommend these methods because we've tested them across hundreds of websites and know what works. And what works is asking prospects to take action: calling, requesting an appointment, or providing an email address for future follow-up.

Getting People to Call Your Law Firm

If you think that prospects are going to pore over your website to find a phone number to call, you are sadly mistaken. People want easy access to information, and they want to find it where they expect it.

What this means for you is that, in order to get your phone to ring, you need to have a few elements in place. The phone number that you use on your website needs to be the same number someone would get from 411. You should not use a 1-800 number on your website unless it appears below your actual office number.

 WARNING

Using a tracking number on your website or anywhere online can have a dramatically negative effect on your rankings if not implemented correctly, leading to your website falling off the face of the earth. See the chapter about local directory listings for more information about your phone number and address. Never use a tracking number without a trusted professional coding the proper javascript on your website.

The first step is to put your phone number in the upper right-hand part of your website. This phone number needs to be text, not a JPEG image. Lots of web developers and companies will take the easy road and add an image of the phone number on the banner (or upper part) of the website. The problem is that a prospect cannot click on that image from a mobile device to call your firm. More importantly, search engines can't read images, so they'll completely miss your phone number. Make sure that your number is easy to read on your website and on a mobile phone.

You should also put your phone number and address in the lower right-hand side of the website, or at the bottom. This way, if someone is reading your website and ends up at the bottom with the inclination of calling you, your number is easy to find. Once prospects decide the design and information of your website are enough for them to feel comfortable calling you so they can give you their business (money), you need to make it extremely easy for them to do so.

As the "About the Attorney" pages are some of the most visited on your website, it is sometimes beneficial to add a phone number on each attorney profile page—especially for firms that like to have a direct dial number to each lawyer. Finally, your phone number needs to be on your "Contact Us" page. This is where you can add a fax number, extensions, office number, and any other numbers you think people may want to call.

"Tell Us about Your Case" Opt-In Form

The "tell us about your case" form is one of the best conversion techniques for a law firm today.

It is easy to think of several moments when a prospect might not be comfortable picking up the phone and calling your firm. If someone is about to go through a divorce and is at work doing research during his or her lunch hour, the last thing he or she is likely to do is pick up the desk phone and say, "Yeah, I am going through a divorce, and I need an attorney." However, that does not mean that the prospect is not ready to contact you.

By providing a place for prospects to ask you to contact them later, you are giving them an option to remain quiet about their situation until they are in a place where it is appropriate to talk.

The best way to get a prospect to request an appointment is to put a simple, clean, well-designed form on your website. A nice bonus to the request an appointment form is that it can separate prospects into two categories: those you want for your firm and those you would prefer work with someone else.

Here is where your request an appointment box should appear:

See *Figure 28.*

Figure 28: Example of an appointment request box

The form serves both as a filter and a great marketing tool. Ask prospects to give you the following information:

- Name
- Email
- Phone
- Legal issue or comment

After they submit the form, you should be re-directing (sending) them to a page on your website, alerting them that their message has been received and that you will contact them shortly. Then, you or an administrator in your office receives an email with the person's contact information and details regarding his or her specific situation.

Because you ask for a few details, you get the chance to see if the prospects are a good fit for your firm before you even talk with them on the phone. This will save you both time and money. If they are *not* the best fit, you can have your admin recommend them to someone else. If they *are* a perfect fit, you can set up an appointment right away. Using a request form really helps you prioritize online leads.

Can I Please Have Your Email Address?

Certain practice areas require a longer sales cycle: estate planning, business, some real estate, or even adoption. Sometimes, people are not ready to contact you by phone, are not in an appropriate place to make a phone call, or are not inclined to schedule an appointment; however, they may still be interested in your firm. You don't want prospects to close their browser and forget about you. There are opportunities for you to capture their email address and reach out to them later, when they may be more ready.

People know about spam, they know about scams, and they're hesitant to give out their email or phone number to just any site they find on the Internet. (That being said, people are more willing to give out their cellphone number today than ever before, as many use their cellphone number as their primary or only number.) You have to overcome that initial hesitation and get them to give you their information.

If you have a regular publication, like a newsletter, you can highlight that on your website as somewhere people can go to get regular information. Similar to the appointment form, this would be a small box that offers the option to receive follow-up contact. You can add a title like "Get the latest adoption updates" above a box that asks for their email address.

If you follow all these steps, anyone who signs up with his or her email will be a "warm" lead: a warm lead is someone who is going to be very receptive to your business. These leads will be easier to convert into clients because they've shown an interest in your services; they've already done the hard part, which is getting in contact with you. However, you have to act on this; warm leads, like anything else warm, tend to cool over time. This leads us to our next item of interest: your follow-up process.

Follow-up Process

Follow-up strategies are vital to any Internet marketing strategy, and it's equally vital that you automate them as much as possible. Many firms will try to follow up manually, but the overhead required isn't feasible for most firms. Don't spend time fielding emails and responding one by one. We've had clients in the past that sent out email newsletters every week. When new people came in, they would be manually added to this email list. That sort of system may work in the beginning, but it's easy to see that it doesn't scale well at all. You need an automated method of follow-up that both preserves quality and also scales up well, thereby freeing resources and keeping your Internet marketing strategy running smoothly and efficiently.

Follow-up Framework

First, we have to talk about the framework for follow-up. When we talk about follow-up, we're not talking about people that come in through the door, necessarily; we mean new prospects that resulted from traffic to your website. You need a follow-up strategy whether or not the contact is initiated by phone, email, or online via your website.

When new prospects get to your website and choose to give their name, phone number, and email address, they go into your prospect funnel. These prospects have gone to the trouble of giving you this information, so they're warm leads: they are obviously interested, and you have to get to them fast before they cool off. Your funnel is the resource where you capture your leads and market to them specifically from there. The whole function of the funnel is to enable you to respond quickly to whatever communication the client happened to initiate.

The best way to ensure rapid responses is to set up a basic auto-responder system. This system will provide two things: 1) it will alert you when prospects have given you information, and 2) it will send them a message immediately. The most traditional and common auto-response is an email, and that's something they should be getting immediately.

Follow-up systems will send a boilerplate email you create to anyone that fills out a form on your website. These emails should be unique to the place the prospect requested information. If the prospect is looking for an appointment, the email reply from your automatic system should reference that you will contact him or her about the appointment request. If the prospect asks to receive your newsletter, the email should confirm that he or she has been added to your newsletter list.

There are a number of automated follow-up systems that are used by many firms: tools like Constant Contact, Infusionsoft, and MailChimp, among others. Depending on your area of law, there are some services that even provide dozens of pre-written email templates that have been proven to help convert email prospects into clients. Whichever service you select, you have to make absolutely sure that it has a system capable of capturing information, storing the information in an organized way, and making it as easy as possible to send out automated responses.

WARNING

One important note: make sure that you own the emails in the follow-up system and that you can easily export the email list at any time, which will give you the freedom to move between vendors. This is especially important if you utilize a service that provides email templates for your area of law.

In addition to your automated email responses, you should also implement a strategy for phone numbers. The reason for this is that the Internet is open 24 hours; it doesn't close, and your website is happily receiving visitors all around the clock. Your office hours, however, are only during the day, and even with the best intentions, you won't always be able to answer your phone at ten in the evening. If someone gives you his or her phone number, you should not only email that person right away but also email someone in your office with the person's information and interest. When your staff members get in the next morning, they can see the email and know that a prospect tried to get in touch. They can then pick up the phone and say, "Hey, this is Bob Jones from Jones, Smith & Johnson. I see that you have a legal issue and I'm just calling to ask if there's anything we can help you with."

This is an example of a very personal follow-up to a warm lead—with an emphasis on the personal. We can't stress that enough: you are a local business providing a service to the community, and you need to reach out and make personal connections as fast as possible. The bigger the step, the better, and an automated email is the minimum bar to entry.

There are even companies that provide answering services outside of normal business hours. However, these services are typically not staffed with attorneys who can answer legal questions. The service is there to provide a human for the caller to interact with, keep the lead warm, gather a little more information for you, and set up some type of follow-up with your firm. For the faster-paced sales cycles, like personal injury, DUI, or other criminal matters, this is a great way to prevent the prospect from calling the next competitor he or she finds in the search results if that prospect only gets your voicemail.

It's vital that you have a stable, reliable follow-up system in place so that you can call leads within minutes of them submitting a form. If you can get to your prospects within five minutes, you know they're an extremely warm lead, you know they were on the website, and you know they are interested. People who filled out your form are much warmer leads than those who just happened to see your name in a direct mail piece or a local flyer.

- To get found on Google by potential clients, you need a functional website.

- If your website doesn't convert visitors into actual clients, it's pointless!

- Simpler, more functional websites get more people to call or email than "flashy" websites. (Less fancy does not—and *should not*—mean bad design.)

- Your website is your first impression online; a bad website is damaging to your firm's image and won't garner you any conversions. A good website is professional, functional, and attractive—not poorly designed, cluttered, or confusing to navigate.

- Your website's layout should include a homepage, "About Us" page, "Practice Areas" page, blog, and contact page.

- Each page of your website—and especially your homepage—should use consumer advocacy copy, which is copy that illustrates how you can solve your potential clients' problems and how they can benefit from hiring you.

- Remember the 2-20-2-20 rule for earning your prospective client's time and attention on your website.

- Include strong calls to action throughout your website to get people to call or give you their information. You should have your *real* phone number (as text) in the top right-hand corner and a request an appointment form on each page.

- Your Internet marketing funnel is the place where leads enter and you market to them. People enter your funnel by giving you their information, such as their email address or phone number, via your website.

- To have your Internet marketing work as smoothly and efficiently as possible, you need to automate some of your follow-up systems. The systems should scale well and preserve quality; manually capturing, organizing, and following up to every email just isn't feasible.

- Set up an auto-responder system, which will both alert you that someone has contacted you and immediately respond to that lead. When prospects email you, they should get an email in return. If they give you their phone number, someone from your office should know to call them.

- Services that provide auto-responders include Constant Contact, Infusionsoft, and MailChimp.

- You can also send out periodic newsletter emails (summarizing your blog posts) to everyone on your email lists.

- It's important to have follow-up systems in place in order to provide personal service and make sure that your firm is at the top of potential clients' minds. Even if they don't need your services now, they may need them in the future—and you want them to think of you.

Chapter 6:

Creating and Managing Your Blog

Google has made one thing clear: you must have quality content if you want to get ranked. One great way to add quality content to your site is through blogging. It also provides you a place to regularly talk to your community about the services you provide.

Blogging has become a powerful force on the Internet. It also has a distinct advantage for your law firm in that it's by far the easiest, most convenient, and most effective way to add new, updated content to your website. You don't have to change your website copy all the time, you don't have to deal with static pages, HTML, and minor edits; you just have to update your blog consistently.

You have to have a blog on your website. There is no option. Google has emphatically stated that they're going to give stronger ranking credit to re-sources that are both relevant to the website and the most current. This makes sense, given the overall makeup of the Internet: new content is replaced often, and newer information is frequently far more helpful than old information to a person searching. This is why blogging is so important: it is absolutely, positively all about making regular, useful updates to keep your site current, relevant, and full of useful content.

"Okay, I get that I need a blog," you're thinking. "Now what?"

In this chapter, we're going to cover the what, when, and how of blogging. We explained earlier why your blog belongs on your website. But how often should you blog, and what should you write about?

How Often Should You Blog?

You have probably seen blogs of other law firms. Some publish a post on their blog every day, and others update their blog only when the stars align. You might be wondering if the amount that you publish to your blog matters.

We're here to tell you that it does matter—kind of. A good rule of thumb is this: do not create a blog and then only post once every four months; you will look like you are either out of business or simply lazy. There is a right and a wrong way to go about blogging. Why? Google prefers steadily updated content, which means that you should be blogging at a minimum of once a month. Honestly, you do not need to blog every week anymore.

Each blog post should be between 1,000 and 1,500 words long. A post definitely shouldn't be any shorter than four hundred words, or Google may deem it not useful. There are people that say you are free to blog how ever long you want; they say that you should ignore the search engines and that you should blog because it builds a strong brand. There is some truth in this statement. You can also put a billboard in the middle of the forest if you want, but I wouldn't recommend that.

This may seem daunting to you—and understandably so: the thought of composing another written piece that is 1,000 words or more isn't appealing to many people out there. If you truly think about it, however, once or twice a month isn't too bad; if you make a schedule and stick to it, you'll find that blogging really isn't the chore you thought it would be.

You must blog consistently to achieve the positive results you're after. If you blog twice one month, skip three months, and then write four posts the next month, you are not going to see positive results. This is because Google and other search engines only crawl (or look at) your website every so often. If they crawl your website and don't see anything new, they move on to your competitors. If they crawl your site and see tons of new content that week, they give you a point for the new content, whether it's one piece or four.

If you're finding that you have time to write more often, try adding more community pages or deeper practice area pages. There is no reason to focus all your new content on blogs, but this is still a valuable tool in your marketing efforts.

Some people go into blogging with a very linear mindset. They think that since two is better than one, five must be better than two. It's not, and you'll experience a diminished rate of return in this regard. Two blog posts a month is better than one, but five blog posts a week is barely better. The bottom line is this: if you're blogging more than twice a month, there are other and probably better things you could be doing with that time.

What in the World Do You Write about?

Having a blog is all well and good, but a blog without useful, relevant content is hardly a blog at all. Now that you know how often you should blog, we'll cover what you should write about.

Your blog is not the place to try to hard-sell every person that visits your website. Being overly self-promoting will have a very negative impact on your blog: no one will want to read it.

If you are funny, be funny. If you are serious, it is acceptable to be serious. We recommend that you write in a style that fits your personality. Here are the three main content points you should hit on in your blog:

1) **Talk about What You Do**

This one may seem pretty obvious, but it's worth mentioning: talk about what you do, not who you are. Don't talk about yourself, how long your firm's been around, or how great your service is; this isn't going to help you at all. To put it bluntly, most people simply do not care all that much about these things. And even if they do, they don't want to read about them on your blog.

Instead, your blog should be filled with quality content that relates to the services you provide. Quality content is valuable or useful to the user. For example, let's say you're an estate planning attorney, and a new law affecting testamentary capacity was recently passed. A perfect blog post would cover the law and the information that people interested in estate planning need to know. The title could be, for example, "Just Old Age, or Dementia? How to Know if Your Parents Are Legally Able to Make a Will."

2) **Plugged In: Talk about Local Events**

While the first point may seem obvious to most, this isn't. This is a super secret content creation method for Internet marketing. The trick is this: talk about local events. Simple. Blogging about things going on in the community and tying them back into what you do is a fantastic way to gain local credit with Google and other search engines.

You could, for example, blog about a big event in your city and how it relates to your community. Let's say you live in a college town, and the town quadruples in size every Saturday during football season. Are you proud of or frustrated by the big event? Do you think it's good or bad for business? Think the traffic isn't worth the amount of money the game brings into the town? Do you have suggestions for parking or must-visit restaurants for the inbound football fans? A blog post like this will indicate to readers that you're a part of the community you live in and will give Google lots of keyword clues about your community, helping you to rise to the top in your location.

How do you find out what's going on in your area? Visit your local news or city website. Find the local events section, click on the story about the event, and use the content as a starting point for your post. You can also quote several lines from the news source. Make sure to always include the URL (website address) of the story. And when you add the URL, be sure that it links back to the news website. This will help Google see not only that you are talking about something local but also that the story is being validated by a reputable source.

Furthermore, don't feel pressured to make the local blog post about legal issues in the community. In fact, shy away from it. These local community posts are as valuable in their own way as the legal-related posts you make. Someone browsing your website and blog will have plenty of time to see your other posts and find out about what you do. With a combination of local and legal blog posts, you'll get ranking benefits from both your location- and industry-related keywords.

Community-based blog posts also have the added advantage of making you seem more likeable and down to earth. When potential clients find your blog, it will be beneficial if they get not only practical legal knowledge, but also some connection to you. When they read your blog, they won't see just another faceless attorney; they'll read your blog posts about the community and think, "Wow, this person has personality. They seem to really know what they are talking about, and they also seem to be really invested in my community."

As a result, they'll be more likely to pick up the phone and give you a call, and you just got a warm lead by being a personable blogger who talks about the community!

3) **Use Other Websites as a Resource**

Similar to curating content from the local news, you can also find content from other bloggers, news websites, or associations that are talking about issues related to your specific practice area. Many websites, from *The New York Times* to the *ABA Journal*, offer great articles about your legal practice area. If you have friends in other cities that also practice your area of law, you may want to curate some of their content. They may feel flattered that you took the time to talk about their blog. In turn, they may do the same for you, building you a stronger overall web presence.

When curating content from other websites, the best practice involves quoting only a couple of sentences at most and always linking back to the source. Note that it is not good enough to link to the main page of the other website; you should link directly back to the actual post where you found the information.

See *Figure 29*.

How Do You Write?

We see the same mistake on too many law firm blogs: writing completely in legal jargon. Why do so many attorneys do this? There are two reasons: 1) they are used to writing in legal terms, and 2) they don't want to sound unintelligent to their peers.

Figure 29: Example of a blog post that refers to other content

However, you don't have to sound like the smartest person on the planet on your blog. Of course, you shouldn't be sloppy in your writing, but you shouldn't sound like a king preaching from atop an ivory tower, either. Google likes to see content and blog posts from normal people; conversation, stories, and anecdotes are all things it likes to index, so conversing on your blog makes you more reachable and more indexable.

Furthermore, this isn't just a Google-specific tactic. More importantly, potential clients will be turned off by a blog filled with legal jargon that they don't understand; if your potential clients don't get what you're talking about, they won't find it useful. And as a result, they won't be persuaded to hire you. Your potential clients will find more conversational, informal posts appealing, so make sure to write them that way. Remember, they came to your website from an Internet search because they are trying to solve a problem—don't confuse them even more.

It's always been a good marketing strategy to be likeable; it's the age-old concept that people are more likely to work with those similar to themselves. They will see your blog posts and think, "Hey! This guy knows what he's talking about and likes what I like." They will see a real person, which will make them feel more comfortable with the idea of working with you. It will greatly help your sales when prospects feel that they know you more personally.

There is no set rule. Your local posts can be a little shorter than 1,000 words, so try to pepper those in throughout the year. A healthy blog will have four or six local posts every year.

This tactic may feel a little too touchy-feely for some, but don't knock it; it works very well, and blogging is a great way to do it. It drives clients and will improve your ranking, which is, of course, a major goal of this book. We've had clients that have followed this process to the letter, and their specialty posts about law gained only a few hits and comments. It was their local story blog posts, however, that became a focal point; conversations about how bad traffic was when a big event happened got tons of links, comments, and opinions from across the board.

In the end, this is what you want. It's the reason for this section and the reason you're branching out into the community. Not only do these posts with local keywords mean big index boosts from Google (a goal of this book), they also mean very effective general marketing. They make you a real person that people feel comfortable calling—one of the best advantages you can have in our modern, very skeptical era.

What Else Should You Include on Your Blog?

When blogging, don't forget to add images to your blog posts. Images attract the reader's eye and can drive people to click. Because you will want to have your blog posts appear on your social media networks, the images you choose should be at least 500 by 300 pixels in size.

There are lots of places online where you can get royalty-free images, which you can use on your website without having to pay anything. However, the best thing to do is take the images yourself. You likely won't always be able to take your own images, though, so use a combination of images you find online and your own.

Pictures grab people's attention. Do not just pick any random image. Make sure to put some thought into how people may react when they see the image.

See *Figure 30.*

There are many benefits to blogging that go beyond the SEO component, including establishing your firm as an authority on your practice area(s). A blog allows you the opportunity to educate and share your knowledge with your market. It is also beneficial for building your connections in the local community you serve. Yes, having a blog can drive a lot more business, but that should not be your only motivation for having a blog.

Figure 30: Example of a blog post. Note the use of a large image.

- Blogging is important for a number of reasons; it benefits your search engine ranking and helps portray your expertise to your prospects.

- You should blog, at a minimum, once a month.

- You should blog about events at your firm, things going on in your community, and current news that you can relate to your practice areas. Blogging about both legal and local events will give you the opportunity to use all of your keywords.

- Write in a way that the average person can understand, not using legal jargon. If you blog using too much jargon, it will often turn off prospects.

- Be sure to include images in your blog posts, especially if you plan to use social media to share your blog posts.

Chapter 7:

Mobile Websites and Mobile Search

During our CLE events, attorneys are always asking us if real prospects actually use mobile devices to search for law firms. This is certainly a valid concern: you don't want to focus time and energy on a medium that isn't being used.

By the Numbers

Over the last four years, we have observed traffic to our clients' websites, accounting for hundreds of thousands of clicks. We also collaborated with a competitor that provides web services to attorneys, and they corroborated our data. As it turns out, at the time of this writing, over 29 percent of all traffic to law firm websites originates from mobile phones. That's nearly one-third of all visitors. Depending on the demographics of your target market, this number can get to over 40 percent.

There is no question that, in 2015, your website *must* be mobile responsive. Too many visitors are coming from mobile devices, too many people are trying to get directions or call your firm, and too many search engines are expressing preferential placement for mobile-ready sites.

Mobile devices are rapidly becoming the primary mode of interaction with the Internet. Even way back in 2012, according to the Pew Research Center, 63 percent of adult cellphone owners used their phones to go online[3]. These numbers have only been increasing every year with access to the Internet via mobile devices surpassing desktop access midway through 2014. The mobile revolution is here.

---

[3]   http://pewinternet.org/Commentary/2012/February/Pew-Internet-Mobile.aspx

You read that correctly: more people now access the Internet via mobile devices than desktop computers. Moreover, mobile is already a driving force behind many of the search engine changes we've seen. Google is setting up its local search infrastructure with a heightened focus on mobile because it believes users will continue to increase their searches on mobile.

Mobile search is a different creature than traditional search and requires a different approach. Users who search on a mobile device used to be driven by the "I need something right now that's near me" mentality. This is in contrast with desktop users, who have been more willing to sift through websites and Wikipedia articles in their research. Very few people were willing to do that on a mobile phone; most likely, they were looking for a business nearby that they could walk or drive to quickly. Now, that mentality is changing.

More and more, as people are at lunch, driving around, sitting at home, or talking, they're thinking to themselves, "Oh! I'll just use my phone to search for a quick answer." The same applies to people who are just sitting around, eating dinner, or watching TV at home; chances are, they have their iPhone, Android phone, or tablet sitting right next to them. Instead of waiting to look up the answer to their problem on their computer, they'll just pick up their mobile device and look up the answer right then and there.

This is great news, even for attorneys (although many attorneys have looked skeptically at us when we've said this). The fact that the mobile search mentality has changed to include more research-oriented problem-solving means that you can now get in the mobile search game and expand your website's reach. This might seem far-fetched, but it's actually not; think about your own mobile phone use or the usage patterns you've observed in others. There's a clear aura of instant gratification with any sort of mobile device, and users take advantage of this to get immediate answers.

If your site is not mobile-friendly, or your Google+ Local page is non-existent (Google+ Local is extremely mobile-friendly), you're going to get left out in the cold when it comes to getting prospects on mobile.

Remember when we said that mobile search requires a different approach? Because of space constraints, the mobile realm tightens up the ranking requirements quite a bit. On regular desktop Internet, you've got to be in the top seven listings; it's preferable to be in the top three or four, but seven is the bare minimum. On mobile devices, however, if you're not in the top two, you're not being seen: very few people scroll down on mobile phones, and often, they simply tap the first or second result they see. This is important to you because mobile phones offer an unparalleled ease of use. For example, many phones like iPhone and Android offer built-in calling from the web. Users can simply tap a finger on your phone number, and the smartphone dials the number automatically. As mobile devices become more and more common, it's critical that your site be mobile-friendly and in the A or B spot of Google's local search returns so that it's seen by as many prospects as possible.

See *Figure 31.* -Because mobile is only going to increase in importance, you should start thinking about your firm's mobile strategy. The two essential areas that you must focus on are mobile search and how your website looks on a mobile device.

Mobile Search

The two biggest players in mobile operating systems are Apple (iPhone) and Android (pretty much everyone else). Until recently, these two systems shared most of their search and map functions with the same online reference centers. This meant that a user searching on an Android phone would be getting the same results as a person with an iPhone. Well, all of that has changed, and with that, you need to have knowledge of and a strategy for two separate operating systems.

So how do you get ranked on a mobile phone?

Getting Ranked on the iPhone

Over the last couple of years, we've seen many changes to mobile devices. In the most stunning change, Apple broke away from Google Maps entirely, creating its own Maps app (mostly powered by Tom-Tom and Yelp). This app features local search with "Info Cards," navigation with turn-by-turn directions (spoken by Siri), interactive 3-D views, and Siri integration. (Before this change, Apple was using Google Maps integrated with Siri.)

In the new Maps app, users can type in a local search or can ask Siri to do a local search for them. On the results page, the user can see the results or tap a pin on the map to see the business's Info Card. This Info Card will have the name, address, phone number, and website (if there is one) of the business.

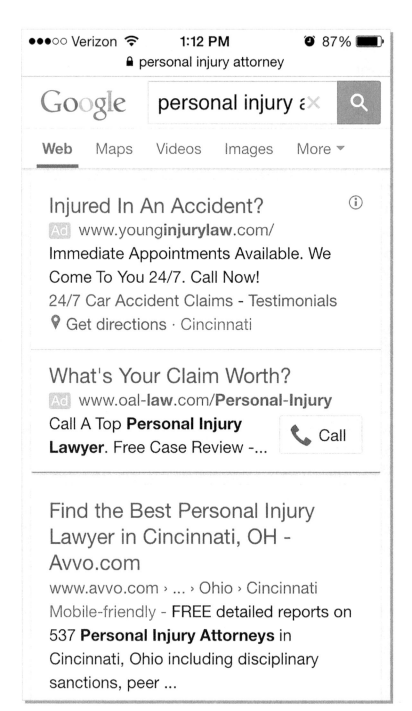

Figure 31: : Google search results on a mobile smartphone

On the card will often be local business ratings and reviews from Yelp, as well as photos and deals.

While Apple has not officially disclosed the directories that they are using to populate their business listings, their copyright page acknowledges Acxiom and Localeze[4]. According to Apple's iOS 6 presentation by Scott Forstall, Apple, in 2012, "has already ingested more than 100 million business listings around the world" for its local search.

Now is the time to start caring about these changes and about mobile search, if you don't already. It would be very unwise to ignore this development from Apple; millions of people in the U.S. (and around the world) use iPhones. (In 2013 and 2014, Apple sold more than 100 million iPhones, according to data from Apple reports.) And now, iPhone users utilize Maps to do local search and get turn-by-turn directions to every search result, bypassing Google completely.

To prepare for and compete in this game, you'll have to make sure that your business is listed correctly on Acxiom, Localeze, and Yelp. This is only a start, as no one knows yet if these data providers are the exclusive providers for Maps. If your business is listed incorrectly (or worse, not listed at all), you could lose out on a portion of potential business by not showing up in the search results of Apple Maps.

In addition, you should be adding photos to your listings and working to encourage happy clients to leave positive reviews on Yelp; these reviews are now an integral part of Maps and may play a part in where your business is ranked in Apple's search results. Photos and reviews will also make your Info Card more attractive to potential customers. (This is true not only of Maps, but of Google+ Local as well.)

Getting Ranked on Android and Google Search

Even though Apple's release of Maps changes the game a little bit, that doesn't mean that you can abandon Google. Android has more users than iPhone and is still powered by Google. Also, many iPhone users of Safari

---

4   http://gspsa21.ls.apple.com/html/attribution.html

browser still search using Google. In fact, all the same rules apply for Android and Google; if you follow the previous chapters on getting ranked locally and using the right type of SEO for your website, you are already 90 percent of the way to getting ranked highly on an Android device. The only addition you need to make is focusing on Yelp and Localeze to include Apple. By including Yelp and Localeze in your focus, you will be ensuring that you have created listings on the appropriate local directories for Android and iPhone.

One recent addition to Google mobile search is that Google has created guidelines and tools for a website's mobile search readiness. Furthermore, Google is starting to add the term "mobile friendly" right in the search results on a mobile device. Starting in mid-2015, we expect Google to start adjusting the ranking of websites on mobile devices to give preference to those websites that best meet their mobile guidelines. To see how your site measures up, have your webmaster give you the Mobile Usability report found in Google Webmaster Tools[5].

See *Figure 32.*

Creating a Mobile-Ready Website

Your mobile-ready website needs to be easy to read, navigate, and use. This feat is not so easy on such a tiny screen, compared to a 15-inch monitor. The biggest conversion killer on mobile is having a site that the user can't see or use well. Think about it: have you ever visited a website on your phone and couldn't read any of the text because the words were too tiny? Or worse, the site didn't pull up at all? We've seen it all, from websites that look terrible to websites without a phone number that you can click to call the business (another killer of mobile website conversion).

In the development world, both tablets and mobile devices are considered mobile. For some sites, the website design from the desktop is suitable for a tablet or iPad. Take this example. When used on an iPad, this website is easy to read and navigate: See *Figure 33.*

---

5   [https://www.google.com/webmasters/tools/mobile-usability]

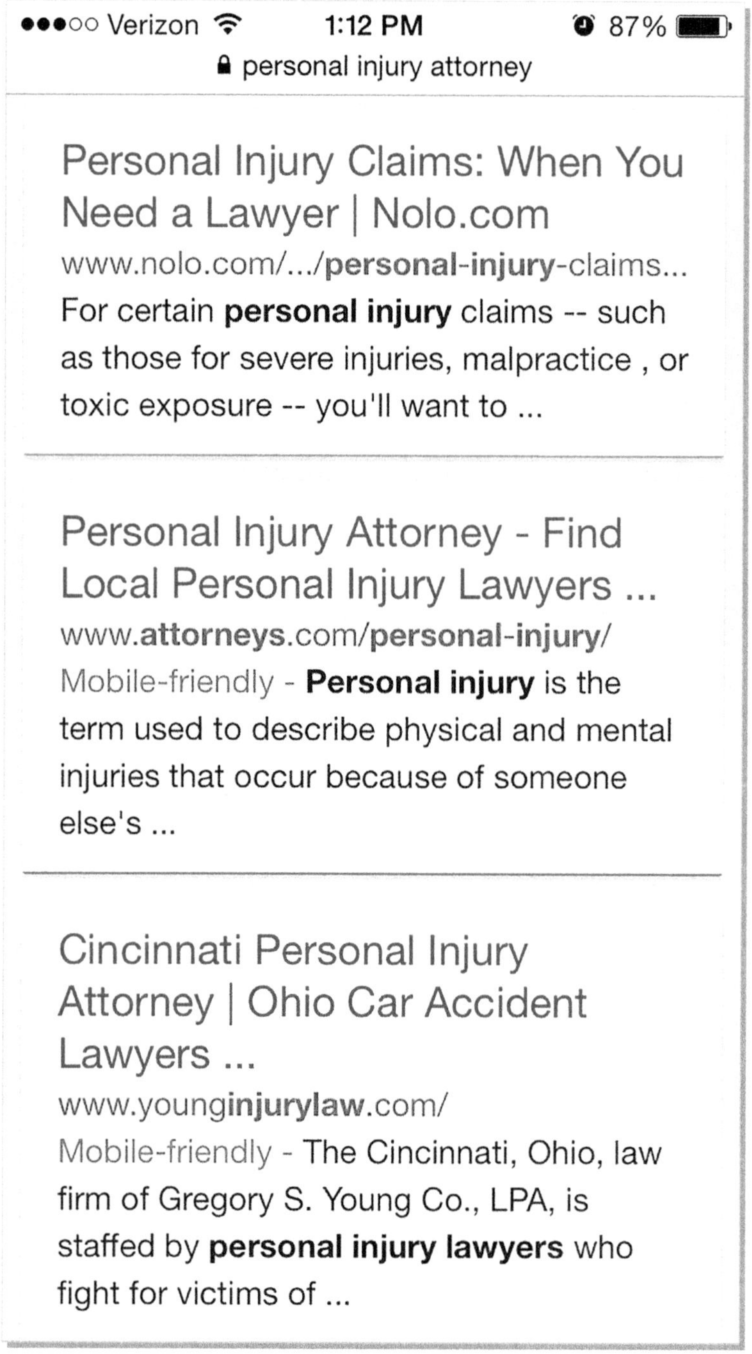
●●●○○ Verizon
1:12 PM
87%
personal injury attorney
Personal Injury Claims: When You Need a Lawyer | Nolo.com
www.nolo.com/.../personal-injury-claims...
For certain personal injury claims -- such as those for severe injuries, malpractice , or toxic exposure -- you'll want to ...
Personal Injury Attorney - Find Local Personal Injury Lawyers ...
www.attorneys.com/personal-injury/
Mobile-friendly - Personal injury is the term used to describe physical and mental injuries that occur because of someone else's ...
Cincinnati Personal Injury Attorney | Ohio Car Accident Lawyers ...
www.younginjurylaw.com/
Mobile-friendly - The Cincinnati, Ohio, law firm of Gregory S. Young Co., LPA, is staffed by personal injury lawyers who fight for victims of ...

Figure 32: Example of mobile friendly search results on a mobile device

Figure 33: Example of a website viewed on an iPad

When it comes to preparing your website for mobile, there are two main options for your firm:

1) Responsive website

2) Mobile-friendly website

We will cover both options; however, note that in 2015, we believe you will need to move your website to a responsive design. Not to get overly technical, but search engines consider mobile load time (the amount of time it takes a user to view the content of a website after clicking on the link) to be an important factor in rankings.

It takes 0.6 seconds for a mobile device to call the server and request that a website be shown on the device. A mobile-friendly coded website does what is called a "redirect" to the specifically designed mobile website. This takes another 0.6 seconds to call the servers again. Google has said that it would like to see a mobile website load in less than one second. As you can see, a mobile-designed site already takes 1.2 seconds in server call time before the website has even started loading.

Responsive, on the other hand, does not require a redirect and thus can load the entire website in less than one second. This is why we say that you will most likely need to create a responsive site this year.

Responsive Websites

A responsive website auto-adjusts the layout and copy on the website to match the size of the screen available. If you view a responsive website on a mobile phone, it will be in one long column with big buttons. If you look at that same website on a tablet or laptop, the site may be three columns with smaller buttons.

Creating a responsive website requires certain coding to be put into place in the architecture of your website. This is most likely not something you will be implementing yourself. Asking your webmaster to handle this is the most advisable strategy for creating a responsive website.

One disadvantage to a responsive website is that it does not allow you to organize your content as easily for optimization on a mobile device while maintaining ideal optimization on a desktop. This snafu is caused by the nature of how a responsive website compresses your website layout. It takes a very talented web engineer to create the proper code so that the correct elements of your mobile site are visible in the correct places.

Responsive websites do have advantages, however. These include the ease of updating and having one solution that encompasses mobile, tablet (iPad), and desktop compatibility. Because a responsive site is just a compression of your current site, any changes you make to the website are automatically added to the mobile version. Thus, you only need one solution, as opposed to three separate solutions.

See *Figure 34.*

As you can see from the image, responsive design prepares you for various device sizes. When Apple and Samsung roll out the next "phablet," you won't have to worry about your website rendering properly because the system auto-adjusts to the screen size.

Figure 34: Example of a responsive website

With almost one-third (and growing) of your traffic coming from mobile, the conversation about whether you should or shouldn't have mobile is over. There is no option—you must have a mobile responsive website.

- Nearly one-third (and sometimes more) of all traffic to law firm websites comes from mobile phones. If your website is not mobile responsive, you are missing out on all of these prospective clients.

- More people now access the Internet via mobile devices than desktop computers.

- Many search engines are expressing preferential placement for mobile-ready sites. Mobile is already a driving force behind many of the search engine changes we've seen, especially those from Google.

- On mobile devices, if you're not one of the top two search results, you're not being seen: very few people scroll down on mobile phones, and often, they simply tap the first or second result they see. You need to be in the A or B spot of Google's local search returns.

- Don't focus your efforts on just one mobile operating system. You need to rank on the iPhone *and* on Android.

- Your site should be mobile responsive. It should load in less than a second and should auto-adjust the layout and copy to fit any size of screen.

Chapter 8:

Maximizing the Yield of Your Online Activity

You can stop trying to get a crystal clear method for measuring the exact ROI of your online efforts (or marketing efforts in general); it is just not possible to get one perfect number. That is not to say that you shouldn't measure things, try and calculate cost per lead, and set up an intake process to capture the right data—you should just be using this information as a leading indicator so you can adjust your strategy along the way.

An integral part of growing your practice is understanding how to manage your prospect flow and track your online yield. For all you know, you might be overspending on activities that only generate a small amount of activity. Even if you are getting a high volume of new clients, it could be at too high of a cost. On the other hand, you might not be spending enough on marketing. Just a small increase or reallocation in your marketing budget could dramatically increase your client flow.

In a typical advertising budget—which we've seen from many clients we've worked with—the vast majority of dollars get spent on ads in the yellow pages, on the radio, and on TV. Most attorneys are not spending enough money online, and if they are, they're paying for an extension of the yellow pages (which is usually not tracked well and is often very ineffective).

Advertising online has a huge advantage over traditional advertising methods typically used by most firms: it's extraordinarily easy to track what's happening throughout the entire online process, from who emailed you, to what's in the funnel for leads, to what's going on with your analytics, and so forth. This is very difficult to do with regular advertising. Quite often, the only method of communication that traditional advertising media gives a firm is the potential client's phone number or website. Unless you ask each person where he or she heard about you or create a unique phone number for each ad (which is, by the way, a very good practice—more on that later), you're not getting very good information at all regarding how your advertising budget is helping you.

In contrast with traditional advertising methods, marketing online can give you amazingly vast amounts of data. You can track how many people visit your website and what keywords they typed in that led them to find your website. If they visit your Google+ Local page, you can track who visited, when, and how. Some directory listings have tracking data in place, but the big kahuna in the realm of tracking is Google Analytics.

Google Analytics is an absolute must-have for your website. If it's not already on your website, ask your webmaster to integrate Google Analytics with your site. If he or she can't, it's time to find another webmaster. That's how important Google Analytics is to your understanding of how effective your website is. This tool tells you where your visitors are coming from, how well your website is converting leads, how long your clients stay on your site, and more. See *Figure 35.*

Figure 35: Google Analytics

Because of the extensive amount of data that Google Analytics gives you, it's an unquestionably essential tool for monitoring your website. Some of the important metrics to pay attention to with regard to your Google Analytics are:

1) **Time on site:** How long is each user staying, on average, on your website? This time needs to be a minimum of one or two minutes. If the time spent on your site is too low, you will not achieve high rankings, or worse, you could have a serious conversion problem. Possible issues that can cause low time on a website include the following: there are too many busy graphics, it is too difficult to navigate, the topics on the site don't match what was searched, there is too little information about the prospect's needs, the website is unattractive, or it takes too long to load the website.

2) **Number of visitors:** How many people visited your website over the last week, month, and quarter? Don't get bogged down with daily numbers; think about your overall traffic in weekly chunks. Whether you get more or fewer visitors is a key indicator of your ranking. Ranking higher will lead to more traffic, period.

3) **Pages visited:** What pages do people navigate to, and what pages do they leave your website from? You can see the pages they visited and get an "exit" percentage. If you find that people tend to navigate to a random page, like your attorney profile page, and then leave, you may have an issue on that page that needs to be fixed. The issue could be bad copy, bad graphics, or a long load time. If you find that people navigate to your contact page and then exit, that can be assumed as normal human behavior, and there is likely no issue present.

4) **Traffic source:** From where and how do people get to your website? This is crucial to understanding what websites are driving your traffic. Are people coming from search engines, an email campaign, LinkedIn, Google, or Twitter? This information helps you know where to focus your efforts.

Of course, there is a lot more data in Google Analytics that is very useful. These are simply the top four places to get started. If you can master these four areas of your web presence, you will be way ahead of your competition. These areas of Google Analytics will arm you with the information you need to make educated decisions about where to spend your time and money, as well as what needs to be fixed (if anything).

In addition to Google Analytics, another great tool is Google Webmaster Tools. This tool is beneficial specifically because it tells you the following: what pages Google has indexed on your website, how many people are linking to your website across the Internet, the number of impressions your site is getting in Google search, and the times that people are clicking on your link when you show up in search engines. All of this information tells you how well your online marketing strategy is doing overall. This should be complemented by statistics on your email funnel and auto-responders, which should track how many people are getting and opening your emails.

We mentioned before that having different phone numbers for each ad is a good practice, and even this is more easily tracked online. There are services that allow you to create unique numbers that all forward to your actual phone number; the only difference is that the call statistics are available online, and you can see at a glance how many calls each number received. This isn't to say that you have to get rid of your current phone number—in fact, you shouldn't. These numbers are only forwarding numbers and nothing more; clients with your old number can still get through perfectly fine.

The only applications for tracking numbers should be: paid advertisement, promotional pieces used online or offline, and on your website when someone visits from a search engine. Remember that you should never use a tracking number on a directory listing. You can use tracking numbers on your website, but please make sure to have a seasoned local marketing/web developer code the javascript that is required to do this correctly. If done wrong, it can hurt your web presence.

On top of everything else, there's your own internal CRM (customer relationship management system): how much money you're charging, how long you're working, how long you spend with each client, etc. As we'll see, a CRM is an incredibly key resource in determining your total yield from online sources.You can use generic business CRM platforms, like Salesforce.com, Infusionsoft, and Microsoft Dynamics, or legal specific CRM systems, like Avvo Ignite and Captorra. This is so important that we added a new section to this version of the book. The final section covers practice management, including CRM systems.

You can track almost anything online in order to measure your online presence, and if you're going to take anything away from this section, it should be this: it's imperative that you have a strong, stable, well-defined system in place to correctly track your leads. Most law firms believe that they have a good process in place, but when it's subjected to a rigorous examination, it turns out that it breaks down. Of course, it's good that they even have a system in place, as it's common sense and standard marketing practice. They're spending money, and they want to know where that money's going and how that money's helping them. To have an effective online marketing strategy, however, you need to go above and beyond; you need to be taking in the data that shows you the point of entry for all your clients.

When tracking your leads, you need to know the following important information: the source of your new clients, the value of each client, and the amount you're spending on each of your marketing strategies. With this information, you can more accurately calculate your yield.

Very often, we end up having to build new systems and processes for clients to ensure that their reporting is accurate. Make absolutely sure, when planning out your overall online marketing strategy, that you decide what metrics you're going to use and exactly how you're going to track them.

Efficient and accurate monitoring in this realm gives you an unparalleled advantage over firms using only traditional media. It's important to note that achieving positive yield from your online efforts does not happen in the first month. Getting to a position where your site is fully optimized and getting traffic from the right places takes at least six to nine months. Your overall strategy should focus on a multi-year approach. While we don't give specific numbers from our client work, in averaging some of the most successful firms we have worked with, here is an example case study to show this. In the first year, Smith, Jones, and Carter Law Firm invested $85,000 in their web presence. In the second and third years, they focused on content, link building, and maintenance, investing another $48,000 per year. Over three years, their CRM tracking tools showed they netted 394 new clients with a lifetime value of $3,200 each, for a total of $1,260,800 in gross revenue. They have shown from their data that each new client, on average, results in 0.15 of a referral, equaling an additional 59 clients over the three-year period. This brings their total revenue from online activity and the additional business that was generated to a grand total of $1,449,600.

Now you can see how investing $181,000 over three years is a worthwhile investment, with almost $1.5 million in gross revenue.

BIG TIP

If you're working with an outside agency, you should absolutely require them to provide you with reports on your website activity. They can get them, and if they are not giving them to you or if they claim they're unable to get them, there's something seriously wrong; they're either hiding something or they're simply not as good as you thought they were.

What these reports need to cover is how much traction your web presence is producing. This should include your various conversion opportunities.

While the marketing agency you hired should provide you with online data, your firm will be responsible for determining how many people call you because of your website. When prospects call your office, you should ask them how they found you. If they found you on the web, ask them where (Google, Google+ Local, Yelp, Avvo, etc.). This practice—in conjunction with any tracking numbers you use—is the best way to track phone calls from the web.

Once you have a good understanding of the general yield your online strategy is producing, you can start to look at ways to further maximize that investment. One great way to do this is to take advantage of paid web re-marketing campaigns and paid social media campaigns. These campaigns allow you to drop a cookie on a prospect's computer browser when he or she visits your website (or section of your website); then you can specify ads about your firm and services that will follow that person around the Internet or his or her social media accounts for a set period of time. You may have seen this with ecommerce sites; you research a product and then you see that product referenced everywhere you visit on the Internet for the next two or three weeks.

What this does is extend the dollar you invest in online marketing a little bit further by allowing you to try to get a conversion from someone who already took the time to search the web, find your site, visit your site, but left on their first visit without a conversion (a phone call or web form). The great news is that the online advertising platforms (like Google Adwords and Facebook Ads) are quickly getting very sophisticated and you can re-target someone who visited your website based on other demographic and psychographic factors like age, income, location, hobbies, and interests. If you have ever bought an offline postal mailing campaign list targeted at a set of zip codes or other sources, imagine being able to do a similar targeted ad online but only to people who have already visited your website.

- You should be tracking your yield from your Internet marketing so that you know if the money you're investing is actually working for you. Tracking your yield lets you know how well your online presence is working as well as what issues, if any, need to be fixed.

- Internet marketing has an advantage over traditional advertising (e.g., radio and TV) because its ROI can be much more easily tracked.

- Google Analytics and Google Webmaster Tools are must-have tools for your website. Using these tools, you will be able to track metrics—like visitors' time on site, number of visitors, pages visited, keywords used by visitors, and traffic sources—helping you determine the overall effectiveness of your online presence.

- In addition to statistics on your website, you should also have statistics on your auto-responders, including how many people receive and open your emails.

- You must have a working internal customer resource management (CRM) system in place before you can accurately measure your yield. The CRM should measure how much you charge, how much time you spend on each client's case, etc.

- If you choose to work with an agency for your Internet marketing, they should be able to give you a report of your data. If they won't—or can't—something is very wrong.

- Your online presence will take at least six to nine months to get you where you want to be in terms of traffic and conversion. Successful Internet marketing takes time and persistence and lasts for years, not months.

SOCIAL MEDIA

SECTION 3:
SOCIAL MEDIA

CONTENT SHARED ON GOOGLE+ INCREASES DISCOVERY/INDEXING

500 MIL TWEETS / DAY

75%
LINKEDIN USERS HAVE A COLLEGE/GRAD DEGREE

LINKEDIN USERS AVERAGE > $50K IN INCOME

GOOGLE+ HAS 300 MILLION UNIQUE VISITORS MONTHLY

USERS AVERAGE 8 HOURS PER MONTH ON FACEBOOK

FACEBOOK 1.35 BILLION
TWITTER 284 MILLION USERS

PINTEREST

WELCOME TO OUR LAW FIRM

INSTAGRAM

WELCOME

YOUTUBE

REACHES MORE U.S.

ADULTS AGES 18 - 34

THAN ANY CABLE NETWORK

MEETUP

3.03 MILLION MONTHLY **R S V P S**

THE BIG FOUR

FACEBOOK

TWITTER

GOOGLE+

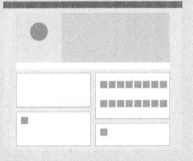

+1

LINKEDIN

ADVANCED TACTICS

ONLINE
NETWORKING

FACEBOOK PAGES POST ADS

+300%
TRAFFIC

INFOGRAPHICS

TARGETING
SPECIFIC PROSPECTS

ENGAGEMENT

This is usually the point where you zone out, lose interest, or skip past this section because you might be saying to yourself, "Other people can worry about social media, I have no need for this information."

Competency, at a minimum, is necessary for the success of your online presence.

There is also the fact that your prospects and clients are using social media in their everyday lives. People are not casually using social media; they are using it at a staggering rate. Over 500 million tweets are posted per day, there are one billion active Facebook users—need we go on?

The truth is, you need to understand how social media works to accomplish two goals:

1) Competently advise your clients or staff about social media activities and how they can impact situations.

2) Reach your prospects in the space where they are spending time.

We know how silly Twitter (and other social media platforms) sound. We've seen the derision it has received from all sides, including our friends and the media. But don't laugh just yet.

We are going to cover what social media means to your rankings, how it functions, why it matters, and where you should focus your efforts. Note that this is one area where you specifically need to check with your bar association to ensure that you are completely informed of your state regulations, as they may differ from this chapter's information.

Why Social Media?

From a marketing perspective (we will get to competency later), social media has become a very powerful force. It also impacts how Google determines what is relevant online. In order to game the system and get ranked on Google, the Internet has become full of bots, scammers, article spinners, and links to irrelevant or otherwise spammy articles. Social media, however, does the vetting by itself. Users of social media sites aren't going to share spammy links with each other; they're going to share real content. As a result, Google has realized that indexing and calculating relevancy from social media is very beneficial, as social media (in general) is comprised of real people posting real content—content that was valuable enough to warrant a "Hey, check this out" from one person to another.

Many people still try to avoid social media for whatever reason, be it concerns about privacy, general lack of interest, or what have you. The statistics on social media and Internet marketing, however, can't be denied:

- The average annual income of LinkedIn users exceeds $50,000 per year, and three-quarters of users have a college or grad school degree.[6]

- Facebook, as of Dec. 2014, had 1.35 billion monthly active users. To put that into perspective, that means Facebook has more than three

---

6   https://www.quantcast.com/linkedin.com

times as many users as the U.S. population; this is very important in terms of saturation.[7] Also, the average Facebook user spends about 8 hours per month on Facebook.[8]

- Twitter has more than 284 million active users (as of Dec. 2014)[9] that send more than 500 million tweets per day.[10]

- Google reports that 300 million people per month globally visit Google+, and the content shared on g+ increases discovery and indexing.[11]

These statistics show you that social media is an extremely influential force in today's cultural mind-set, and it's only getting stronger. Social media is here to stay. More and more people are joining every day and getting recommendations from their friends and family about great services they received.

Google has been taking notice of this and responding accordingly—and so should you. In this section, we're going to take a look at social networks and your strategy for each of them. We're going to figure out just how to approach these social media websites and use them to help Google notice your firm.

Before we jump into the individual uses for each network, we need to cover the basic functions of each so you can competently advise your clients and staff.

7   http://www.statista.com/statistics/264810/number-of-monthly-active-facebook-users-worldwide/

8   http://www.nielsen.com/us/en/insights/news/2014/clicks-and-balances-top-government-websites-and-us-web-brands-in-february-2014.html

9   http://www.statista.com/statistics/272014/global-social-networks-ranked-by-number-of-users/

10   http://www.internetlivestats.com/twitter-statistics/

11   http://bits.blogs.nytimes.com/2014/02/19/the-loyal-users-of-google-plus-say-it-is-no-ghost-town/?_r=1

Competency: How Social Media Works

This section is designed to give you the basic information you will need to know about the functions of each major social network: Facebook, Twitter, LinkedIn, Google+, Pinterest, and Instagram.

We hope it doesn't come to this, but if you are headed into court and need to know more about how social media works, feel free to reach out to us. We would be happy to give you insights that pertain to your specific situation. Simply contact expert@gngf.com with your question.

A great example of social media incompetency in the courtroom occurred during the George Zimmerman trial. Attorneys from both sides examined Jenna Lauer in an attempt to ascertain her connection on Twitter to Zimmerman's brother. In the video, it is obvious that neither attorney has a clue how Twitter works, thus each attorney was unable to confidently say whether she was or was not connected to this individual.

There will also be moments where your clients will need guidance on how to avoid making mistakes when posting on social media channels during litigation or other legal scenarios. For these reasons and more, it is essential that you understand how social media works.

Facebook

How do people connect on this network?

Facebook is what we call a two-way connection. In order to be connected to someone, both parties need to accept the terms. When two people connect, they are referred to as "friends," and both people can see what each other posts.

The default privacy settings are important to note. It is advised to set the privacy settings to "private" (meaning only your friends can see your activity). You will always have the option of changing a post to "public." If you want to do this, all you have to do is select the public option from the drop down menu.

There are two types of accounts: personal and business pages. These two types of pages are separate from one another. See *Figure 36* & *Figure 37*.

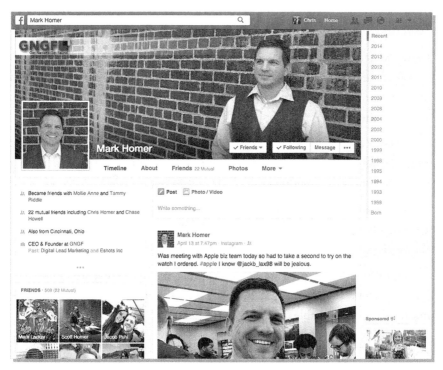

Figure 36: Example of a Facebook personal page

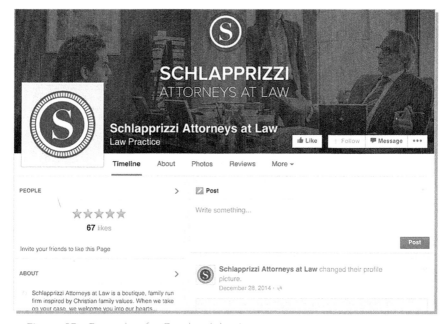

Figure 37: Example of a Facebook business page

Twitter

How do people connect on this network?

People are able to follow anyone without permission. That makes this a one-way connection. People can follow you, but that does not mean you are following them.

When a user follows you, they can see all the things you post on your stream. The only way to send private messages requires both parties to be connected and use something called a Direct Message (DM).

Users should consider everything they post on Twitter to be public; just ask a number of the politicians that accidently thought they were communicating privately.

A great way to look at Twitter is analogous to a microblog. You post messages on Twitter for all your followers to see. When people you follow post information, you are able to see it in your stream. See *Figure 38*.

Figure 38: Example of a law firm's Twitter page

Terminology you should know about Twitter:

- **Tweet:** The message you post.

- **Retweet:** When someone reposts a message from another user to all their followers.

- **Direct Message:** A private message sent between two people that are following each other.

- **Followers:** People that are following you.

- **Following:** People that you are following.

- **Tweets:** Total number of tweets sent by that user.

- **Hashtags** (#): Used to anchor a tweet to a topic. For example: "Check out our new blog post on #law #marketing at http://www.gngf..."

- **@ symbol:** Used to mention another Twitter user in a tweet. It also acts as the reply function if you are trying to reply to a tweet.

LinkedIn

How do people connect on this network?

There are multiple methods people can use to see your information on this network. People can follow users without their permission and see their updates, discussions within groups, and posts on LinkedIn's content network.

There is also a two-way component to this network. Users can connect with you when both parties accept the terms. This allows them to see your information, message you, and view your full profile.

You can set your privacy settings to limit the amount of information people can see on your profile. However, paying LinkedIn users are able to see all user profiles. The paying option on LinkedIn is a way around viewing restrictions.

Typically people do not post personal or sensitive information on this social network; most users are here for professional reasons. That does not mean someone cannot post personal information on his or her LinkedIn wall, but this information should be considered public. See *Figure 39*.

Company pages and personal pages are not completely connected on this network. You will need a personal account to create a business page, but that does not grant other users access to your personal information.

Figure 39: Example of a law firm's LinkedIn page

Google+

How do people connect on this network?

With a unique connection mechanism, Google+ acts like both Facebook and Twitter. People can follow other users without their permission, and users can also connect with each other.

Information published on this network is indexed by Google within the search results, making it easy to find online. All information posted on this network should be considered public.

Users post information on a wall. Even though you are able to designate your post to be sent to specific groups (called circles), that information can be easily shared. This is why we recommend you consider it public in all cases.

See *Figure 40*.

Terminology used with Google+:

Circles are essentially buckets into which users put connections. These can have custom names. When you want to follow someone, you put that person into a circle. Some people will add you back and also put you into one of their circles.

+1 is the way users "like" a post. This can be done even if the users are not connected on the network.

Pinterest

Pinterest is almost exclusively used to share images. People post images to their "board," which acts like a virtual cork pin board. All information posted on this network should be considered public.

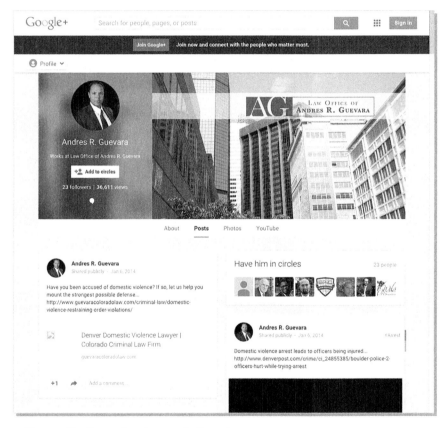

Figure 40: Example of a user's Google+ page

- Social media will be a powerful force in how Google determines what is relevant online.

- Users of social media sites aren't going to share spammy links with each other; they're going to share real content. As a result, Google has realized that indexing and calculating relevancy from social media is very beneficial.

- Statistics show that social media is a growing influential force in people's daily lives.

- If you've been avoiding social media, it's time to throw in the towel. Your law firm *must* be on social media in today's digital age.

Chapter 10:

As mentioned, there are currently four main players in the social media game: Facebook, Twitter, Google+, and LinkedIn. This isn't to say that you should ignore the other social media networks out there; they're still important, and in fact, location-based social media platforms like Foursquare/Swarm and Facebook Places are very useful too. You may want to have a presence on those in addition to other minor social networks that we will discuss in the next chapter.

For the core of your marketing strategy, however, we're going to focus on the big four. This focus will give you the most coverage and best exposure to potential clients.

Facebook

Most of your clients and prospects know and use Facebook, so you're going to need to capitalize on that. A lot has changed in the last year with regards to how a law firm should use Facebook. The first thing your firm needs to have is a business page. This is completely separate from your personal Facebook page.

Your personal account and business page are entirely distinct. People who are only connected to your business page cannot see your personal information or posts.

Many of you may be worried by Facebook's privacy settings. But you should know that your business page is *not* your personal page. It's not connected to your personal page, it's not the same thing as your personal page, and nothing you post on your personal page will appear on your business page (and vice versa). They are completely separate entities. For those of you who are resisting joining Facebook or are afraid that your business page will expose your personal page, fear not: none of your personal information will go on your business page, and your privacy is safe.

If there is information that you do not want the public to know, don't post it online—anywhere. Just ask the multitude of people, including various politicians and celebrities, who have regretted posting inappropriate things online.

Your Facebook Page

A page, quite simply, represents your law firm. There are two reasons you need a Facebook page: 1) it gives you a link back to your website, and 2) people will likely expect you to have one. You can use Facebook to grow a fan base, increase your brand awareness, and get new clients.

When it comes to local search ranking and spending your time wisely, it is recommended that you do not put a ton of energy into building a Facebook dynasty. Instead, use Facebook as a linking location and a reputation guardian. After several algorithmic updates by Facebook, there is only one strategy left for truly making this network lead to success: paid advertising. This is important information because it will shape your overall Facebook strategy.

Facebook has a massive target market of the exact people that need your services: divorce, personal injury, estate planning, etc. It definitely has the right mix of people with the money and motive to hire attorneys, and your page on Facebook will be a great place for them to get in touch with you regarding their problems.

Setting up a Facebook page is simple and only takes about 10 minutes. (Because you already have your website up and running, the information is all in one place.)

TO SET UP A FACEBOOK PAGE, FOLLOW THESE DIRECTIONS:

1. Visit the Facebook "Create a Page" page (http://www.facebook.com/pages/create.php) and select "Local Business or Place."

2. Add your firm's information, including your real address and the actual phone number to your office (do not use a tracking number).

3. Set up an account. You have two options here: you can either log in using your personal Facebook account (again, your personal information will not be used on your page; this is just to ensure that you are a real person, not a scamming computer program) or create a new account.

4. Fill in more information about your firm. This includes a description of your firm and the URL to your website. Facebook automatically provides the "http://," which you want to keep. You can add multiple websites here. We recommend adding your blog and Twitter profile as well.

5. Add an image to your page. Select an image that is geo-located. There are two images that are important: the profile image and the cover photo. The profile image is square; the cover photo is more like a banner that is more wide than tall. You can adjust the image size and position after you upload the image.

6. You have the option to add your Facebook page to your account's "Favorites" list and to add a payment method for future Facebook advertising. You can skip both of these if you choose.

7. Your page is now live, so you should complete as much as you can. There are options to add more images and post a status update. Fill in any other areas that you can, including hours of operation, etc.

Here is what the Facebook page set-up process looks like, with screenshots walking you through step by step.

Figure 41: How to create a Facebook page

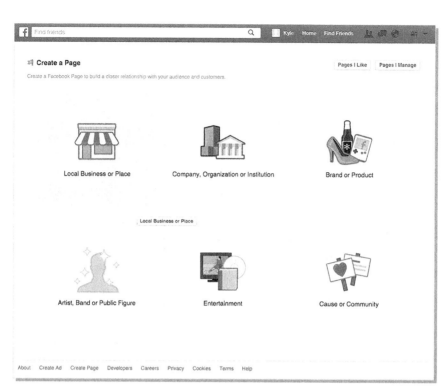

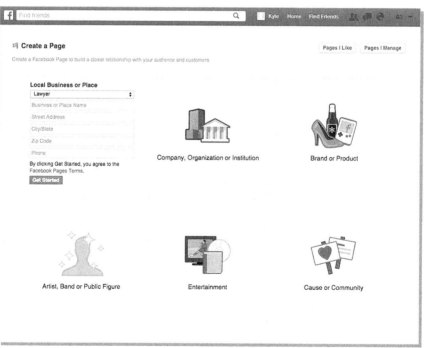

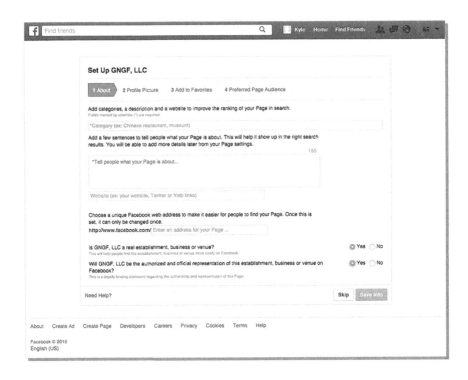

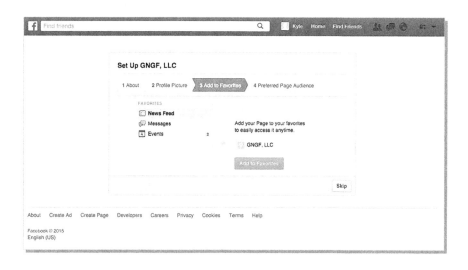

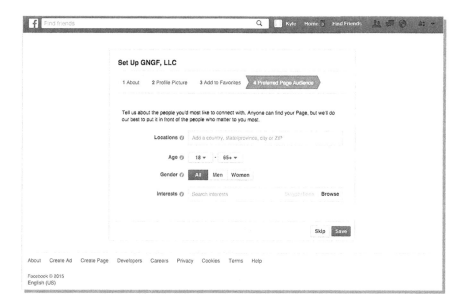

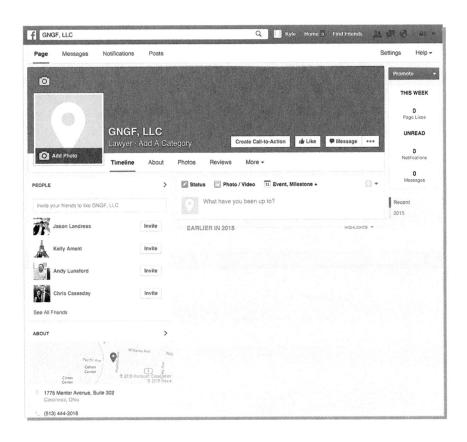

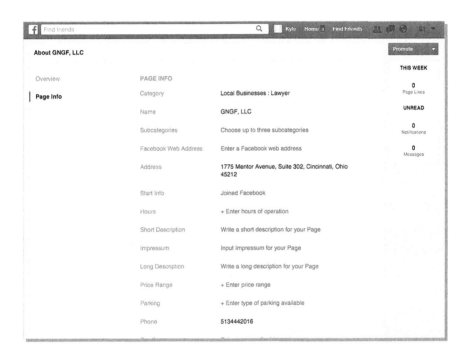

What to Do with Your New Page

Just over a year ago, we would have said that the main focus of your page is merely to create a quality link back to your website, which you already have 50 percent complete because you added your website URL to the Facebook business page. However, now we recommend that you show consistent activity and grow your Facebook page following. A good way to do this is to post a status update with a link to your blog post each time you write a post. You also need to reach out to build a small following.

Don't worry about updating your status on Facebook with what coffee you drank that morning or pictures of your cat. All we are concerned with here is creating a link on your page back to your website content (blog posts, articles, news updates, announcements, etc.).

This is perhaps the most important thing to know about social media in general: all of these pages can be linked together in different ways. There are so many options for managing law firm pages that it's vital that you have a professional who knows how to set up social media accounts correctly. Barring that, you need to get online and do some extensive research into establishing the proper social media channels. This is not something you throw together quickly.

The great news is you do not need thousands of fans on your Facebook page. We recommend you target about five hundre by the end of the year. This is very doable if you are posting new content regularly. A quick way to get some extra fans is to have people in your office post about your firm's new page on their personal profiles, inviting others to "like" your page. Other techniques include adding a link to your Facebook page in your newsletter or email signature and asking new clients if they want to follow your page to stay informed about other legal issues.

As we mentioned before, the best technique for Facebook success is paid advertising. Imagine Facebook as the cheapest billboard you can buy in the exact part of town that you want. For roughly $120 in ad spend, we typically see anywhere from 20,000 to 130,000 impressions. Some of those impressions are turning into website traffic, likes, shares, and comments. Furthermore, with Facebook paid advertising, you can hyper-target the advertising using an alarming amount of specific psychographic and demographic variables. All these things are impossible with a billboard. This is just one of the many powers of Facebook.

Page Post Ads on Facebook

There are several methods for advertising on Facebook: promoted posts, Facebook ads, sponsored posts, and page post ads. For a law firm, the best option for advertising on this huge network is page post ads.

This is not to say that you cannot have success with other types of Facebook ads; we're merely saying that this type of ad will give you the best bang for your buck.

A page post ad originates on your firm's Facebook page, and the ad is placed in the news feed of your fans' friends. When done properly, the ad displays to people that are connected to your fans and people that meet your psychographic targeting. Why is this important? There is a saying that your next best client is only one degree from your current client.

There is another benefit to this type of advertising on Facebook: the cost is much lower compared to your other options. Starting around $100 per month, you can increase your reach, drive traffic to your website, and boost your status on Facebook. This is certainly less expensive than Google AdWords pay-per-click campaigns. We have seen Facebook page post ads that lead to almost one hundred clicks to a law firm's website for less than $100. The equivalent in the Google pay-per-click world for 100 clicks would typically be over $2,000 or more. This type of result comes with increased exposure, top-of-mind brand awareness, and increased likes on your law firm's Facebook page.

Note: You should aim to have about two hundred fans or more before you embark on a page post ad campaign.

HERE IS A STEP-BY-STEP GUIDE TO CREATING A SUCCESSFUL AD:

1. Select a topic that is current, quirky, funny, or controversial.

2. Write a blog post, of between seven hundred and one thousand words, about the topic you think would be interesting. We recommend running the idea past a non-lawyer for verification that it is, in fact, interesting.

3. Add an image that represents the topic. This image must be a minimum of 500 by 300 pixels.

4. *Bonus*: Add text to the image to make it a meme. A meme is an image with text superimposed (examples following). You can create a meme for free online. Just Google the words "meme creator," and you will find several options to choose from in the search results.

5. Add the post to Facebook. Ask a question in the copy of the Facebook post. The image from the blog should upload automatically and be linked to the blog post.

6. In Facebook's Ad Manager (**https://www.facebook.com/advertising**), click "Create Ad."

7. Select an objective for your campaign. We recommend "Boost your posts."

8. Select your firm's page from the drop-down menu. Then choose the post you just created.

9. Select any filters you think may enhance your ad's performance. This is a case-by-case decision, and you should start

by narrowing your ad reach to the people that would be interested in the ad's information. When you start typing categories and keywords into the ad filter, you will automatically get suggestions. Use those auto-generated selections. Try to keep the total possible reach to at least four hundred thousand users.

10. Keep the add as a "CPM" (Cost Per Thousand Impressions).

11. Set your total budget and time limit. We recommend running ads for three days and setting the budget to $100.

Figure 42: How to create a Facebook page post ad

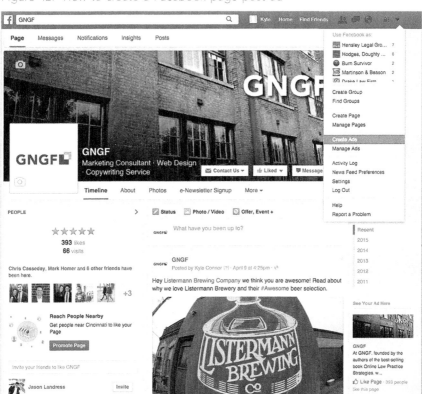

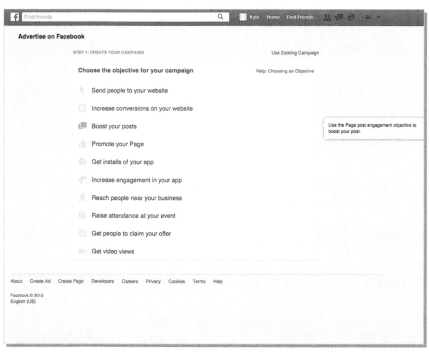

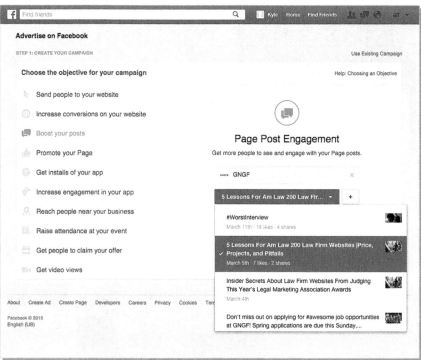

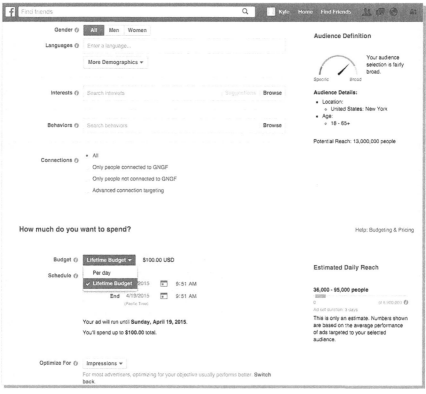

See *Figure 43.*

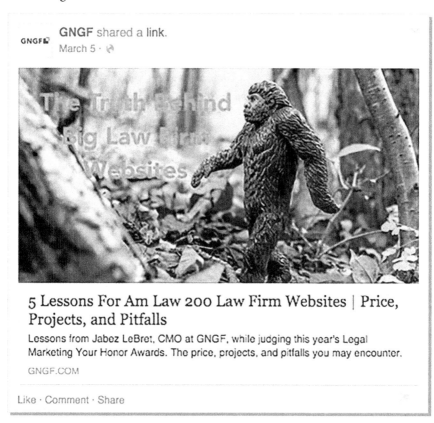

Figure 43: Example of a Facebook ad

Twitter

Twitter is one of the more active social networks and perhaps one that inspires the most reluctance to join. The media and others have vilified it, but the fact remains that Twitter is important.

Why? Every single tweet (a "tweet" is what each individual Twitter post is called) can be indexed by Google and able to be seen by every other search engine. Some social networks, like Facebook and LinkedIn, require a username and password to see most of the content. But with Twitter, there's no requirement to log in to see individual tweets. Therefore, Google can use people's tweets to help gauge the importance of pages all around the Internet. These are called "social signals." Pages and websites with lots of links from Twitter are going to increase in importance. While you don't want to be spammy, you do want to take advantage of this fact.

That's the basis of most of your Twitter interaction when it's all said and done; you can take advantage of Twitter's ability to generate constant content without coming across as being spammy. That being said, you can't just blast out links to your blog articles all day in a stream of useless or irrelevant content. This isn't going to help you increase your online authority.

Like the techniques described in the blogging chapter of this book, you'll want to create tweets (or retweet) about local events as well as current legal content or changes in law—anything that would be important or useful for people to know. Your tweets should be composed of content that is similar to your blog posts but diluted down to 140 characters, and they should be sent out once or twice a day.

Setting up services that automate your social media posts is a quick and easy way to save time, but there is a cost to convenience: posts submitted by these services get less weight with Google and other search engines. For the best and biggest bang for your buck, posting from the actual sites, like Twitter and Facebook, is recommended. Also, be careful of current events and the messaging of your tweets. If a major event like the 2014 Ferguson riots happens, you should take a look at your scheduled messages to make sure nothing could be taken out of context.

Using Twitter may seem as daunting as blogging, especially considering the daily frequency of the tweets. Truth be told, however, 140 characters is not that much at all. Moreover, you don't have to sit by the computer and send them out one by one; there are many websites and programs that let you schedule tweets, including HootSuite (http://hootsuite.com), SocialOomph (http://www.socialoomph.com), and more. You can sit down for an hour and write enough tweets for a week or two, then schedule them and forget about Twitter until the next week, when you sit down to write some more. See *Figure 44.*

Figure 44: Example of a law firm's Twitter page

Try to avoid tweeting duplicate content from your blog posts or articles. Your tweets should be on similar topics as your blog posts, but they shouldn't be copied and pasted straight from the blog unless the tweet is your blog headline. What you can do, however, is link back to your blog from your tweets; this is not only permissible but encouraged. There are website plugins available for countless blogging platforms that enable you to automatically send out a tweet with a link to your blog every time you create a new blog post. Take advantage of these plugins to generate links to your posts. It's a great tool to help you slowly and steadily create links back to your blog. (There are similar plugins for Facebook as well.)

In addition to posting, you should be working to get people to favorite and share your information. If other Twitter users retweet your content, this tells the search engines that not only is the information you shared relevant, but your audience also gives it an endorsement. This would be like a person sending out an email endorsing your latest move into a new area of law. Receiving endorsements from others is oftentimes far more powerful than the things you say on your website or social networks.

In order to get people to retweet your posts, you'll need people to follow you. This is actually not too difficult on Twitter. Type keywords specific to your area of law (e.g., adoption attorney) into the search box on Twitter.

See *Figure 45.*

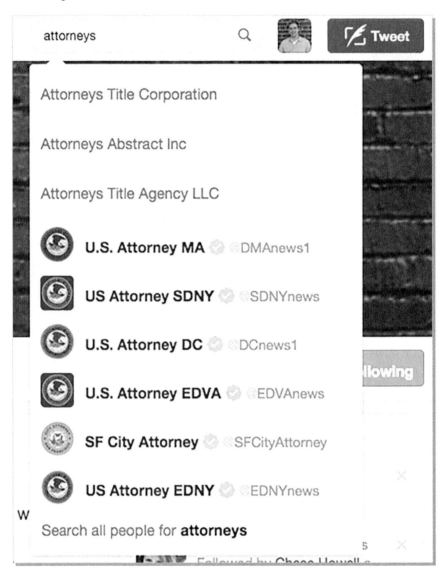

Figure 45: Twitter's search feature

Online Law Practice Strategies

Twitter will give you two types of returns: tweets and people that are connected to that phrase. Select the option to view the people connected with that phrase, and start following people. Go down the list, and start by adding the first 50 people. Then, type in another keyword, and select the first 50 people. Twitter attempts to avoid scammers, so you are limited from adding more than 100 people in a day. Know that it is perfectly acceptable on Twitter to follow complete strangers. Twitter makes it very simple; with one click, you can follow someone.

Now that you're following others, how do you get people to follow you? The two best techniques are interaction with the people you follow and retweeting your followers' tweets. If you retweet one tweet from someone you follow and reply to another tweet each time you log into Twitter, you will be well on your way to building a following.

With Twitter, start slow; don't spend too much time on it. Think about Twitter as something you can do a little every day. In two years, you'll have a formidable Twitter presence. Remember to post your own blog posts as links once or twice a week and tweet about anything you feel would be interesting to your audience—from news stories to comments about the law.

Google+

Google, as a social network, is its own animal; understanding how it differs from the other major social networks is essential. Of course, Google is not just a social network. Today, Google's social network is integrated with its search function.

So, how is Google+ (or g+) different from other social media platforms? Here are the four other major social networks and their differentiating functions:

LinkedIn: Before, you simply posted your résumé. Now, you can collaborate with colleagues and vendors. You can learn and get answers to questions from groups. As the most closed network of the four, you must know someone's email, already have worked with them, or be in a group with them to connect. The publishing platform is unique to LinkedIn.

Twitter: You can tweet information out to many people, and this information can be spread quickly. Google indexes this network, which is a bonus. Anyone can follow your updates. You can follow me, and I do not need to follow you in return. Information is sent out in short bursts, and interaction takes place both on Twitter (in a short conversational style) and off Twitter (follow this link to see this video, read my blog, etc.).

Facebook: The current king of social media, Facebook is about "friendships." You and I must mutually know and like each other to share information. I can post information with the hope that this information is seen on your news feed. There is no guarantee that my information will be seen by my friends. Facebook controls information and uses an algorithm to determine what information it believes I want to see on my news feed. Businesses can participate on Facebook by creating pages.

YouTube: You make, a video. You search for it and can watch, share, and/or comment on videos. As a search-based video network, this is the most open network of them all. Few people use the subscribe function as a social element for law firms.

Why Is Google+ Different?

From a big-picture perspective, g+ is all about connecting all of your computer's uses, both online and offline, in one place. It is like the cloud on a major scale. Google hopes that this will include your documents, spreadsheets, applications, and videos—everything in one location and everything just one click away from being shared.

This has not really worked out the way Google planned, since the network's adoption has been limited. There was a spike in new users when Google assigned g+ logins to all those who have a YouTube or gmail account, but this did not result in a comparable increase in engagement on g+. Since Google owns this network, it certainly has value and is worth discussing.

On g+, you can share all of your information, from your blog to your expense report. But you don't want to share everything with the world. Your friends don't need to know everything about your work, and your clients don't want to know about your personal life. For this reason, Google+ utilizes a function called "circles." Circles control the stream of information both out and in. People you connect with are organized into different circles.

How Do Circles Work?

You can create any circle you want. Examples of circles include "Following," "Friends," "Family," "Work," "Clients," "Very Smart Marketing People," etc. The people you connect with can be in multiple circles. Some people that are "very smart marketers" may also be "friends" and therefore can reside in both circles.

You can choose to send information to one or more circles. This information will appear on the walls of everyone in that circle, or it can be sent as a message. The great thing is that if you share something with your client circle, only the people in that circle—and no one else—see that post on their feeds. Let's say, for example, that you just got back from a family vacation, and you want to share the photos with your family and friends but do not want to bother your clients and the general public with the images: this is easy with circles.

You can choose to see information from one or more circles in your feed. Instead of being told what content an algorithm thinks you would like to see, you can choose the content feed based on your own circles. This allows you to quickly and easily navigate from one set of feeds to the next. Since you can have people in multiple circles, you know that you are seeing what you want from whom you want.

Other Features of Google+

- **Multiple video chat with g+ Hangout:** With this function, you can connect with up to 10 people on live video chat at the same time. The feature is smooth, and the audio is reliable. It's a really great way to connect with people for virtual meetings. The best part of this feature is that the person talking gets the main screen, while everyone else inside the videoconference is reduced to a smaller video box located at the bottom of the screen. This is all done automatically through g+.

- **Easy navigation to all of Google's functions:** While on g+, you can search the web, see your Gmail messages, and access your Google Documents.

- **Simple share option:** Google uses both a +1 button (similar to Facebook's "Like" button) and a "share this post" option for spreading and endorsing content. You should add a +1 button and Facebook "Like" button to your blog.

- **One-click add:** If you see a name in a post, find someone in your friend's feed, or stumble upon someone of interest, you can add them without navigating to their page. When you hover over their name, a box appears giving you the option to add them to a circle. This is a very convenient feature.

Setting up a g+ profile is simple and required for your overall web presence. Similar to other social media outlets, there is an area for information about you, pictures, website URLs, and basic data. As always, only share what you are comfortable sharing. Make sure you take full advantage of industry keywords within the "About Me" section. Like LinkedIn, there is a title area where you should also include keywords about your area of practice.

Posting on Google+

Similar to Facebook, g+ allows you to post on your wall with links, images, or just a status update. There are many reasons you will want to start posting regularly to your g+ page.

To start, this domain is owned by Google. Like it or not, Google is still the largest search engine by a long shot. So, it would make sense that you should post on its own social network. Matt Cutts, a previous member of the webspam team at Google, has said repeatedly that g+ posts do not enhance your ranking. They do, however, rank themselves on Google's search engine. Sometimes, when a post is popular enough, that individual post can be found inside Google's search results.

 BIG TIP

Eric Enge, founder of Stone Temple Consulting (https://www. stonetemple.com/) and widely considered to be the foremost expert on Google+, ran a study measuring the g+ effects on Google rankings. The test was pretty inconclusive, but did produce one interesting finding: using the +1 function on your website seems to get new content indexed faster than waiting for the Google bots to crawl the new content. This is important because getting content indexed is the first step to getting traffic.

More about Circles

Circles act as buckets of contacts. You put your connections into circles, and that controls what information they are able to see you post on your wall. Individuals can be in more than one circle, and you can post to more than one circle.

When you create a post on g+, you select which circles will be allowed to view that content. If you limit this content to one or a few select groups, you will be missing out on the benefit of getting this post indexed by Google's search engine. In order to have your post visible to the search engines, you must select the option to post it publicly along with any of the other circles you choose.

This may seem contradictory. Why not just post to every circle? The best approach is to post relevant information to the people who would be the most interested in that information. This is why it is better to post publicly and to the circles you choose as opposed to posting to all circles.

On rare occasions, the information you post can go to all your contacts. We recommend you keep those posts to a minimum.

It's important to note that there is also a small check box at the bottom of your post that will allow you to send an email to your circles. This option allows you to email the post you make to the people in the circles you have selected. Use this option with extreme caution and reservation. Nothing will annoy people faster than getting regular emails about posts you created on g+. If they want to see what you are doing on a social network, they will likely go to that network.

Sending an email of a post on g+ works best if that post meets these requirements:

- The post is 100 percent relevant to the circle.
- The post requires or seeks interaction from the circle.
- The post is not promotional.

When emailing your circles content from your g+ wall, you want to avoid promotional posts or updates and stick to highly engaging posts. These may include surveys, crowdsourcing questions, or highly charged topics. If you are emailing your posts more than about twice a year, you are doing it too often.

Circles are also a great way to efficiently find the content you want to read. When you look at your news feed on g+, there is an option to view by circle. This will limit the information you are able to see to only the selected circle(s).

Posting content on Google+ should follow the same strategy as Facebook with regards to images, links, and content. It is also a great place to publish your videos from YouTube.

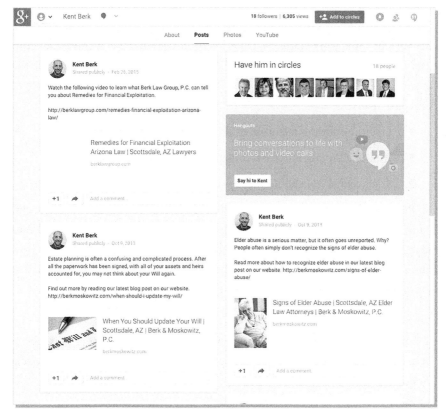

Figure 46: IMAGE 43 - Google Plus Wall.jpg

LinkedIn

The most exciting thing about LinkedIn is the new publishing platform. Before you can start publishing content, you need to understand the LinkedIn user and have a properly established profile.

In social media circles, LinkedIn is often completely overshadowed by its bigger social media cousins, Facebook and Twitter. It is usually regarded as nothing more than a professional or résumé-sharing site. This is a big misconception, as LinkedIn is an enormous resource for prospects if used properly.

To start, LinkedIn itself is no slouch in terms of financial recognition; now publicly traded (LNKD), LinkedIn has a market cap of $8-$10 billion (or $70 to $100 per user), making it a very formidable, fast-growing contender in the social media sphere.

Additionally, LinkedIn has an appeal that isn't related to its market share. Because of LinkedIn's status as a site for professionals, the average LinkedIn user is far more likely to be a potential client; they are more likely to have the means and motive to hire an attorney. The following are the demographics of LinkedIn users:

- Over one-fifth of users are middle management level or above.

- Almost 60 percent have a college or post-graduate degree.

- The average household income of users is $88,573.

Put simply, LinkedIn users are wealthier and have more need for services. Non-useful demographics, like teenagers, aren't crowding the LinkedIn user space to post pictures of their friends and pets. LinkedIn is comprised of your potential clients interacting with each other, looking for professionals, and just waiting to be introduced to your business.

Your LinkedIn Profile

Your LinkedIn profile can ruin your chances of leveraging this entire network. An improperly created user profile will cause you to lose prospects you didn't even know you had.

When setting up your profile, a good rule of thumb to remember is the 2/20/2/20 rule mentioned in the website section of this book. You have two seconds to get people's attention on LinkedIn; once you have their attention, you have 20 seconds to convince them to read more. If they are still around, you have two minutes to earn their next 20 minutes.

Headline & Profile Picture: Your First Impression

The first step is your professional headline and profile picture. Often, you will see headlines that read like a job title, such as "Partner at LeBret Homer & Howell" or "Attorney" and a headshot picture that looks like an outdated picture from the early 90s.

So, how can you get these crucial elements right?

Your headline, which appears right under your name on LinkedIn and is your first impression, should be a thought-provoking, benefit-driven statement about what you do. For example, your headline could say, "Collaborative and Focused Divorce Attorney | Works Toward Mediation Over Litigation."

You will notice that this headline covers what you do ("divorce attorney"), how you do it ("collaborative and focused"), and what it is like to work with you ("works toward mediation over litigation"). When prospects land on your profile, they'll know exactly *how* your job relates to their needs. A headline like this also makes it easier for people to tell others what you do.

When your headline reads "divorce attorney" only, it lacks any compelling reason for a prospect to contact you. As mentioned earlier, having a USP (unique selling proposition) is important to stand out to potential clients. Your headline is a great place to separate yourself from the myriad of other attorneys vying for your prospects' attention and to let clients know what it's like to work with you.

Your profile picture is much simpler: just post an undated professional picture of you. There should not be anyone else in the photo. The picture should be of you, not your law firm's awning. The picture should be from about the chest up, and your face should be clearly visible.

Here is an example of what we don't recommend:

Figure 47: Unprofessional LinkedIn profile

Here is an example of a LinkedIn profile with a simple, professional profile picture:

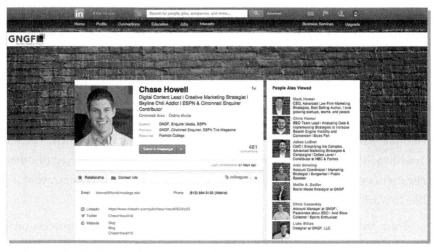

Figure 48: Professional LinkedIn profile

Your Summary

This area is crucial to giving prospects a reason to work with you. Most LinkedIn users will scroll past other information to your summary, so this is where you should concentrate your efforts.

Your summary is your chance to brag. LinkedIn expert and neuroscientist JD Gershbein (http://www.LinkedIn.com/in/jdgershbein) put it simply: "It is easier to talk positively about yourself in the third person than first person." This is a subtle thought with a huge impact. In other words, bragging in first person makes you look arrogant and conceited. Bragging in third person makes you look like a rock star. This is why we recommend writing your summary in third person.

Your summary should read like a biography of your achievements: "[Name] has received [number of] awards and industry recognition for his/her involvement in producing positive results for his/her clients…"

Generally, it is a good idea to keep your summary to three paragraphs or less. It should be organized as such: a summary of accomplishments, the benefits of working with you, and what characteristics separate you from other attorneys.

Endorsements: The New Skills & Expertise Section

LinkedIn has added a section to profiles that is referred to as "Skills." This section was previously known as "Skills and Endorsements," and before that it was "Skills and Expertise," where you were able to type in a list of your expertise(s). This presents obvious ethical issues. This is a great time to discuss the difficulties bar associations are having with keeping up with the rapidly changing social networks and the need for ethical compliance.

In November 2013, the Florida State Bar implied that listing your practice areas in your endorsements section is an ethical violation. We are not here to argue the merit of that decision, but we would like to give you a few options. The New York State Bar issued a recommendation that lawyers not write in the skills and expertise section; however, before the opinion had been released, LinkedIn removed that function. So the New York State Bar added a paragraph just before releasing their opinion also recommending that lawyers refrain from the new endorsements because it included the word expertise. LinkedIn removed "expertise" from the endorsement section, making this recommendation moot.

So what are endorsements good for?

First, check with your state bar to see if it has a rule on the matter. If it has determined that endorsements do in fact violate an ethics rule, log in to LinkedIn, select "Edit Profile," click on "Edit" next to the "Skills" section, and delete the endorsements. Then select the option to "hide" this section from your profile.

We ran a six-month study on endorsements and determined they provide little value. There was no noticeable impact to ranking within LinkedIn for users with more endorsements, there was no impact on ranking better within Google search results, and there was no noticeable impact on the weight of your LinkedIn posts.

About the only benefit to endorsements is making your profile look complete. A rounded out profile with at least 10 endorsements per skill/expertise looks good. This is subjective and only a psychological impact.

See *Figure 49*.

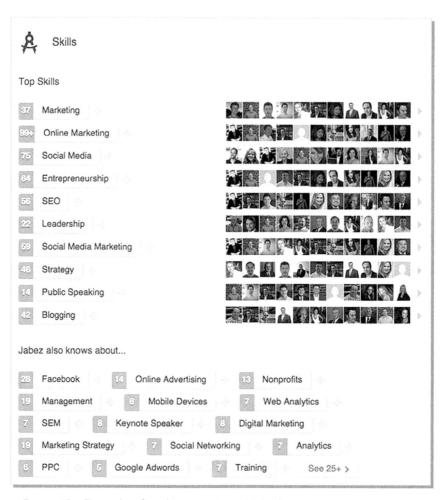

Figure 49: Example of endorsements on LinkedIn

Profile Video

You should have a great video about your firm. The next section, YouTube, is where we will discuss how to create awesome video content for your website. But you don't have to save this video just for your website; you can also use this video on your LinkedIn profile. It is easiest to embed the video from your YouTube account. Typically, the firm overview video works best here, but a content video is better than nothing.

This section is not required on your LinkedIn profile; however, it will drive better engagement. Ultimately, your goal is to encourage people on your LinkedIn profile to take one of two actions: message you or visit your website.

Recommendations

Recommendations are a crucial part of the validation process on LinkedIn. LinkedIn makes this simple by allowing you to send your connections a recommendation request.

We advise that you have no less than five good recommendations. You should send a request to people that you believe will write a compelling recommendation. Remember that you can always delete a recommendation later if it doesn't quite fit your business model or violates an ethical guideline. This feature is useful for complying with ethics guidelines as well. In some states, and as a growing trend, lawyers are responsible for the content of reviews and recommendations that they request. Basically, if you request it, you could be held liable for the content of that review.

We've now covered the basics of a strong profile. Feel free to borrow any elements of the structural layout or style from Jabez's page: http://www.LinkedIn.com/in/jabezlebret.

Connecting with People on LinkedIn

There are three main ways to connect with people on LinkedIn: you and the other person have done business together, you're in the same LinkedIn group, or you have the other person's email address.

LinkedIn is very picky about how you connect with people. The network strongly discourages connecting with random people. That being said, if there is a reason to connect with someone, by all means, do; just be careful about connecting with every person you think would be a good connection. This policy is self-regulated by the LinkedIn community in the form of a spam button. People can and will use the spam button to alert LinkedIn that they do not appreciate your request to connect.

The most important thing to know about connecting with people on LinkedIn—and the secret to almost completely avoiding a spam alert every time—is to connect with people with whom you share a group connection. Also, it is important that you *always* customize the invitation request.

Over the last year, LinkedIn has added the ability to see a list of people that you may know or want to connect with. Included in this function is a one-click option to connect with someone. This feature sends an auto-generated message from LinkedIn: "I'd like to add you to my professional network." This standard request is a horrible, tacky, lazy way to connect with people on LinkedIn. You don't need to write a novel; one sentence will suffice, such as: "We both share a connection with the XYZ group, and I thought it would be nice to get connected here on LinkedIn. Looking forward to staying connected, Jabez LeBret."

Obviously, this strategy works only if you are connected in the same groups. So now, we must talk about joining and leveraging LinkedIn groups.

LinkedIn Groups Can Build New Leads

LinkedIn allows users to create groups to facilitate better connections. These include professional groups, like "Estate Planning Attorneys;" association groups, like "Booth MBA Grads;" and interest groups, like "Dog Owners." This is important to note, as you can build a plan for what kind of groups to join.

WHAT KINDS OF GROUPS SHOULD YOU JOIN?

1) Target joining between 10 and 20 groups.

2) Each group that you join should have 1,500 or more people.

3) The groups should be active (at least one post added per day).

HOW DO YOU TARGET THE RIGHT GROUP TO JOIN?

1) Create a complete ideal client profile. Include age, education, likes, dislikes, professions, and hobbies, or as much information as you can compile. Then join at least eight to 10 groups with your prospects.

2) Find peer groups (anywhere from one to three) that have the most members, and join these groups for access to useful information.

HOW DO YOU SEARCH FOR GROUPS?

You will find a search box in the upper part of the LinkedIn page. This box allows you to search for groups.

See *Figure 50.*

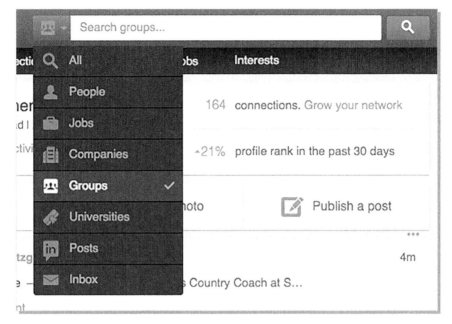

Type in the keywords associated with your ideal client. This search will pull up groups that have similar keywords in their group description. Take a look at the groups, and make sure they meet the aforementioned requirements for joining. Once you decide on a group, click "Join." Some groups require administrative approval to join. Don't worry: it is rare that you will be turned down.

Now that you've joined groups, how do you dominate LinkedIn (in a polite way)?

The main function of groups is participating in discussions. You will see a box where you can add a discussion to the group. We used to recommend that you create discussions in groups to foster engagement. Over the last year, this technique has proven difficult and a poor use of resources.

The best technique for getting results from groups is dominating discussions that are already trending and popular. There is a simple strategy to getting results within groups:

- **Target the trending discussion.** These discussions will appear high in the "popular" section of the group. Look for discussions that already have at least four to six comments before you join in the conversation.

- **Add useful content to the discussion.** Once you've identified the popular discussion you are going to join, start by adding a valuable comment. Your comment should be longer than a few sentences.

- **Comments drive discussion rankings**. A high number of comments posted in a discussion lead to that discussion becoming the number one post. A great tip to increase a post's comments is to provide open-ended questions at the end of your comment. This will drive engagement.

- **Comment on the discussion when other people comment.** Keep responding. When responding to other people's comments, avoid saying just, "Thanks." Instead, say something compelling or something that promotes follow-up commenting.

- **Avoid flat-out pitching.** If you must, invite people to your blog, but do so sparingly. This is a place for information, not a sales pulpit.

- **Comment the most.** You will want to post once for every two or three other posts.

- **The discussion with the most recent and total comments gets emailed to the entire group.** This is huge. Some groups have tens of thousands of members, which means that your discussion could be seen by thousands of prospects. If you get a few comments and post responses to each comment, this is usually enough to push your discussion towards the top.

Responding to Discussion Posts Looking for Your Services

When you come across a discussion that says anything to the effect of "Looking for information on (insert your knowledge area here)," you need to be prepared to market yourself. There will be a ton of people pursuing this client, and you won't stand a chance if you are unprepared or lazy.

When answering these posts, consider the following:

- Research the people. Email them directly, either through LinkedIn or through their website.

- Do not just reply with a comment on the discussion with one or two lines telling the person you are "perfect" or "interested—please tell me more." In fact, don't reply with a comment at all. You should message them directly off the discussion board.

Pulse: Publishing Content on LinkedIn's Content Network

Since LinkedIn has opened up its content network (Pulse) to allow anyone to publish long posts, we began testing and monitoring how to best use this aspect of the network.

First, you need to make sure you have access to publish a post. Go to your homepage on LinkedIn and look for the words "Publish a Post" toward the top right side of the page. Click that link and you will be taken to the publishing interface. See *Figure 51*.

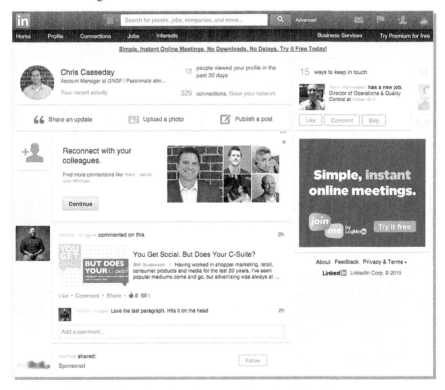

Figure 51: "Publish a Post" at the top right of a LinkedIn page

Now you are able to start writing. Here is a breakdown of the best practices for publishing on this network:

- The type of content you want to publish on LinkedIn is a little different than your blog. This network responds well to topics that include: work related pieces, self-improvement, celebrity news, business topics, and current events. Great topics for law firms would blend your legal knowledge to the above themes.

- Images are a must. The recommended size is 698 x 400 pixels. Your images get published at the top of the article. It is also a great idea to add images throughout the post to break up the content for the reader.

- Your article headline should read like a news article or Buzzfeed piece. Focus on compelling titles that grab your readers' attention. A good example is a piece that Jabez wrote titled "The Art Of Pitching—You're Doing It All Wrong."

- LinkedIn pieces that are longer tend to perform better than short pieces. Target 1,000 or more words per post.

- Avoid using duplicate content from your blog. We've been monitoring this practice and have found that content that is borrowed from your blog—even truncated blog posts—do not get the views that original long form pieces get. This may be a filter LinkedIn is using or the fact that your LinkedIn audience is different than your blog audience. For now, this technique does not seem to be working and should be avoided.

- End the article with a short paragraph describing who you are. Make sure to include links to your website, Twitter profile, LinkedIn profile, and blog.

- The key to successful content is getting your piece to trend. Focus on writing pieces that are well thought out, even if this means posting less frequently. Post your article in discussion groups, inside your LinkedIn feed, on Twitter, and anywhere you can think of to drive more views.

The real benefit of publishing on LinkedIn's network is to boost your profile's views. This spike in activity will benefit your profile's ability to show up in search and, if you set up your profile correctly, lead to phone calls and emails.

Similar to all marketing strategies, this is not a golden ticket. Instead, this is a method for rounding out your marketing efforts.

YouTube

YouTube is the biggest missed opportunity by law firms. At GNGF, we are constantly testing and monitoring various marketing techniques to determine the effectiveness of various strategies. One of our 2014 tests was designed to measure the impact of having video on your firm's website.

As it turns out, video has a huge impact on your website's ability to convert traffic into new prospects. Our study showed an increase of nearly 100 percent in conversions for law firm websites that have a video on the homepage when compared to law firm websites that did not have video.

Interestingly, it does not appear to make a difference if the user watches the video or not; the conversions still go up. This could be due to the fact that having a video on your homepage indicates you are staying current with marketing trends, have put the effort into your messaging, and believe in providing options for the user to interact with your content.

Regardless of why, the fact remains that video works—big time.

There are two major types of videos (and one subcategory): firm overview, content videos, and the occasional video designed to show off your firm's personality.

At GNGF, we created a fun video for Halloween; you can view it here http://youtu.be/0zs843RGnR0. This video gives a glimpse of our personality and gave our team an opportunity to have some fun. It also communicated to our possible client base that we are human and like to do fun things, too. We actually got a call the week after we published the video from a prospect. So don't ignore the fun videos. However, most of your videos will be in the form of content videos, and you will want a professional firm overview video for your homepage.

YouTube has once again become the best place to put your videos. For a while, we were uploading videos to proprietary video networks because Google was allowing for Authorship markup on videos that you placed on your website. With Google's removal of Authorship, YouTube is now the best place for your video content.

People are constantly going to YouTube for answers to all sorts of issues, including legal related topics. From Ted Talks to kittens, this network has become the place for all kinds of video content.

How can you use YouTube to your law firm's advantage? After you have created videos for your firm, you will want to post those videos on YouTube. Because you already have a Google account set up (something you need for your Google+ page), you automatically have a YouTube account.

To upload your videos, log into YouTube using your Google login information. You will want to add your images and branding to the YouTube page. Also, make sure to include a description of your firm. We recommend that you add your standard advertising disclaimer to the bottom of the "About" section.

Uploading videos is easy. There is an "Upload" button near the top of the page that allows you to select the file and click to upload.

Over the last 18 months, there has been a serious decline in the click-through rate from YouTube to law firm websites. Because of this fact, we are recommending that you optimize your video for the "next recommended video."

The first place to start is with the video title. Keep the title short and about the video. Avoid adding your entire location-based keyword phrase (e.g., "Estate Planning Attorney in Lubbock, TX, Talks about Writing a Will"). A better video title would read, "Top Five Reasons to Write a Will Before You Turn 50." The description of the video is where you should add your stronger keywords. The description should lead off with a summary of the video content, then follow with your keywords and a link to the most appropriate page of your website. If you are discussing writing a will in your video, the following example would be a great description:

> People often think that they can—or should—wait to write a will or that creating a will is expensive. The truth is that not having a will can put your family's welfare in jeopardy and later cost your family thousands of dollars. As an estate planning attorney in Lubbock, TX, John Smith helps people plan for the future—giving them peace of mind and helping them avoid difficult situations. If you have questions, call our office. There is no cost to call. You can also visit our webpage at http://www.exampleattorney.com/wills.
>
> This video is for advertising purposes, so please visit http://www.exampleattorney.com/disclaimer to learn more about our law firm's policy on the subject.

 BIG TIP

It is critical to include the "http://" before the "www." to ensure that the link is live. Also, it's important to add your name to the description to improve branded searches and referral traffic. Add several tags that match your topic and location. Try to limit your tags to five or less (with too many tags, you diminish the potency of your optimization efforts). Keeping the tags limited allows you to be specific with the search engines.

Finally, you should select that your video is educational. Don't forget to save the video. It can take a while for a high-quality video to upload, so just leave the window open and be patient.

Once the video uploads, you should post it on your other social networks. With any luck, you will get a little traction on the video. When videos are watched more, they rank higher on YouTube. (Granted, there is more that goes into the ranking, but view count is a factor).

Firm Overview Videos

These videos are a chance for you to talk about what your firm does, what you stand for, who you are, and any other interesting facts about you. Of course, you have about 60 seconds to get this all out.

The video should include the following:

1) Your logo and name at the beginning

2) A combination of interview style and b-roll footage—this is footage that is narrated, but with shots of your office, people working at the firm, your building, shelves of books, conference rooms, etc.

3) A message about who you are, what you do, and what it is like to work with you

4) Finally, end the video with a simple call to action: "So please, come visit us" or "Feel free to give one of our skilled attorneys a call today."

5) Close out with your logo and contact information.

This video then gets uploaded to your YouTube channel and embedded on your home page. Optimal placement for the video depends greatly on your website layout. Since your video is only an element of your conversion and not a direct call to action, it should not take up the best real estate on your site.

On your website, the video should be coded so that it pops out to the middle of the screen. This is often referred to as a "light box." It provides a nice user experience.

Content Videos

Content videos are an excellent way for you to share valuable information with your prospects. Basically, content videos are like short, visual blog posts.

With so many people searching YouTube for answers about everything under the sun, the availability for videos to show up in Google search returns, and the fact that Google owns YouTube, it seems almost too obvious that you should be publishing content to this network as well. For some reason, we are still seeing many law firms passing on this opportunity.

At this moment, law firm videos are some of the most opportunistic, untapped resources available to you.

Preparation is key to a successful video shoot. Typically, our GNGF production crew is able to film 20 content videos in about five hours. We recommend having multiple attorneys on the schedule for the day of the shoot. This will provide variety and present your firm in a better light. After production, the final videos will each end up being approximately 60 seconds long.

Here are the steps you need to take before video shoot day:

1) Break your content into themes based on a couple of practice areas.

2) Create a list of questions for each theme. If you are targeting 20 videos in one shoot, break your questions up with a mixture of frequently asked questions and "should be asked" questions. ("Should be asked" spawn from all those times you find yourself saying, "One thing you haven't thought of with regards to your case/issue/problem is _____.)

3) Write down a brief answer to each question. Do not write a script for each question, as reading a script on camera is very unnatural. Instead you should be answering the question on camera in a relaxed manner. The best way to prepare for this is to have an idea of what your answer is going to be, not the whole answer word for word.

4) Create a light schedule for the day. This should include approximate times for each person participating in the video shoot.

5) Choose your location. Usually, this is a desk, library, conference room, or staged area. If you are not hiring a professional firm, make sure you have ample lighting in the area. Avoid direct sunlight, as this washes out the final video.

6) Review your questions a couple of times before the day of the shoot. Do not stress about memorizing anything, just give the questions a couple passes over so your mind will be ready.

Day of the shoot preparation:

- Get plenty of rest and do not drink alcohol the day before the shoot. This will help you look refreshed and ready. Remember, this video may be the first impression you make on a prospect.

- Dress how you normally dress. Avoid wearing stripes or checkered patterns. They do not film well. Stick to solid colors.

- You do not need makeup, but grabbing a few pads from the drugstore to wipe your forehead and degrease your face will make the final videos consistent.

- Set up the video shoot. If you are shooting this yourself (not recommended), you will need the following equipment: HD camera, 16gb of memory, lighting, microphone, extension cords, tripod, audio capture, laptop, sand bags, 50 mil static lens, and slide mount.

- Shake it out. Go into a room if you need to, but take a moment and get a little crazy. Shake and rattle all the jitters out. This will make the shoot go more smoothly and will make you appear less anxious.

- Have a person sit behind and just off to the left of the camera who will ask you the questions. Answer them as many times as you need to. Try and keep the entire answer to less than 60 seconds.

- Take breaks, drink lots of water, and stay caffeinated.

A professional should handle post-production because it is time consuming and takes special software. In the end, you will have 20 or so content videos. Now it is time to put this content to work for you.

Follow this process for rolling out your new content videos:

1) Get the videos transcribed.

2) Upload one video at a time to YouTube; target two videos per month, for 10 months.

3) Add title and description to YouTube, including a link to your website or a practice area page of your website.

4) Create a page for the video to go on in the resource section, video section, or blog, depending on how your website is set up. Title the page with the video title you used on YouTube.

5) Embed your video on your website.

6) Copy and paste transcription below the embedded video.

7) +1 your video with your Google+ button.

8) Copy your website link (e.g., http://www.samplelawfirm.com/blog/managing-your-trust-accounts).

9) Post your video link on social media channels.

10) Occasionally run a page post ad on Facebook for some of your videos.

11) Repeat until you are out of videos.

If you decide to have an agency manage all of the above, you should expect to pay somewhere between $7,000 and $12,000 for about 20 content videos and one firm overview with rollout. There is no need to pay $20,000 or $30,000 for video production. Also, beware of places that offer all of the above for $3,000. There is no question an agency is cutting corners if they are producing video at that price.

For examples of law firm videos, feel free to visit our website http://gngf.com/services/video-creation/. Here you will find several content videos, fun videos, and home page firm overview videos.

- Your law firm should, at a minimum, have a presence on the big four social networks: Facebook, Twitter, Google+, and LinkedIn.

- Facebook is the biggest social media site. Most of your clients and prospects know and use it, so you must have a business page for your firm.

- On Facebook, your personal account and business page are entirely distinct. People who are only connected to your business page cannot see your personal information or posts.

- Twitter is very important because every single tweet is public, indexed by Google, and able to be seen by every other search engine.

- Create tweets about local events, as well as current legal content—anything that would be important or useful for your prospects and clients to know.

- Google+ is owned by Google, so you should post on its social network. When popular enough, an individual post on g+ can be found on the first page of Google's search results.

- Google+ utilizes a function called "circles." You group people you are connected with into different circles.

- Don't make the mistake of ignoring LinkedIn: as a site for professionals, the average LinkedIn user is far more likely to have the means and motive to hire an attorney.

- Your headline and profile picture comprise your first impression. As a result, they should be professional and appealing.

- You should have no fewer than five good recommendations on LinkedIn.

- Skills and endorsements are sections on LinkedIn that could result in ethics violations. Our typical recommendation to lawyers is to delete and ignore them.

Chapter 11:

Other Social Networks

There are literally hundreds of social networks, and, of course, we are not going to spend time on every one of them. But there are a couple that you should keep your eye on.

Pinterest

This social network focuses on images and provides users the ability to "pin," or post, an image to their own "pin board." Users can also look through images on other people's boards or search for images via keywords.

Pinterest is the fastest-growing social media network ever. This network is also able to boast the largest number of click-throughs (people visiting websites via the images they see). It is comprised mostly of bloggers and women. If either of those is your target market, you should strongly consider getting involved on this network.

On Pinterest, you should be creating content that is useful and in image form. Think infographics or memes (pictures with words over the image).

One of the largest benefits of this network is the volume of clicks you can receive. This is no guarantee, but when you create content that grabs people's attention on Pinterest, they will likely visit your website. See *Figure 52*.

Instagram

This is an image-based social network, like Pinterest; however, it is owned by Facebook and focuses solely on mobile. With mobile use rising so quickly, it is worth exploring the opportunities that may exist on Instagram.

The Instagram application is downloaded on a user's phone. From there, when people take a photo, they are able to put the image through one of Instagram's custom filters that change the look and feel of the picture. Then, the users post the image to their feed. Instagram users can find images on the network through following people or searching via hashtags (similar to Twitter). People can then share that photo by "liking" it on the network.

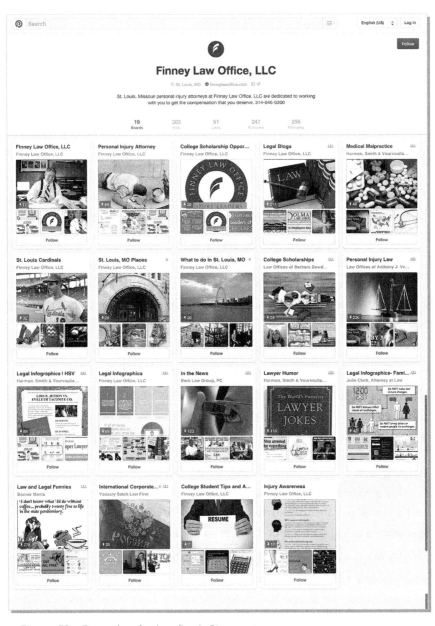

Figure 52: Example of a law firm's Pinterest page

The hashtags you use on Instagram will be important. The maximum recommended number of hashtags on an Instagram photo is five. Moreover, you will see the best results if you are using hashtags that have regional significance. For example, an image of a few attorneys dressed in Roll Tide gear taken from an office in Huntsville, Alabama, may have a caption that looks something like the following: "Getting ready to enjoy the #Alabama #football game - #rolltide go #bama."

It's important to note that Instagram has little use as a traffic generating tool; however, this network can be beneficial from a brand awareness perspective.

See *Figure 53*.

Forums

On forums, the idea is that a group of people get together and share stories and information with like-minded people. There are forums for everything, from cancer survivors to golfers.

When using forums for your law firm, tread carefully. You need to be genuine and thoughtful in the discussion. Before jumping into forums, figure out the characteristics or hobbies of your target market. Then, do a Google search for that phrase with the word "forum" at the beginning of the search. An example would be "forum: wives cheating husbands." In the results, this search will give you forums dedicated to different groups of women talking about situations regarding infidelity.

If you are a divorce attorney, these forums could be a gold mine of prospects for your firm. By thoughtfully participating in these groups, you should be able to accomplish two things: drive traffic to the content on your website, thus building a following online, and get more clients that really need your services.

This environment will require the softest of soft pitches. You should start by contributing to the group and avoid pitching altogether. It's fine to talk about what you do, but keep that to contexts relevant to the group discussion.

Again, we cannot stress enough the importance of respecting both the group and the members of these forums. Do not take advantage of people during their lowest points, and be careful of violating ethical guidelines.

Pinterest is the fastest-growing social media network ever. This network is also able to boast the largest number of click-throughs.

Figure 53: Searching for a hashtag on Instagram

Online Law Practice Strategies

- On Pinterest, you should create content that is useful and in image form, like infographics or memes. (We will talk more about creating infographics in the next chapter.)

- Instagram is an image-based social network owned by Facebook that focuses solely on mobile. With mobile use rising so quickly, it is worth exploring.

- At this time, Instagram has little use as a traffic-generating tool; however, this network can be beneficial from a brand awareness perspective.

- To find forums where the people in your target market might be spending their time, take the characteristics or hobbies of your target market and add the word "forum" in a Google search.

- Forums require the softest of soft pitches. In fact, you should avoid pitching altogether. Instead, start by contributing to the group.

Figure 54: Example of an infographic

Infographics

The infographic has been trending for over a year now. To make an infographic, take a topic, break it down into bite-size factoids, and create a graphic representing the facts with numbers, descriptions, and pictures. (Bonus points are awarded if you can create an infographic that tells a story as well.)

You have no doubt seen infographics, but you may not have known the terminology. Here is an example of one of our infographics: See *Figure 54*.

You should expect to spend no fewer than four hours creating an infographic (and that's once you get the hang of it). There are several tools that you can use to build infographics. A friend of ours—Krista Neher, author of *Visual Social Marketing for Dummies* and CEO of Boot Camp Digital (http://www.bootcampdigital.com)—prefers the website Piktochart (http://piktochart.com/). This is a great resource to create infographics, once you have the content. (Note that we are in no way connected to Piktochart and do not benefit monetarily from its service.) There is a nominal monthly fee to use this tool: $15–$30 a month.

If you or your team does not feel up to the task of learning how to create infographics, you can always hire agencies to create them for you. Prices will range depending on the size, volume of research, and graphic editing that you desire. You can safely budget between $500 and $2,000 (or more) for the entire project.

Picking a Topic

There are a few good ways to determine the topic for your infographic, including mind mapping and connecting your topic to an unrelated, popular topic.

To create an infographic by mind mapping, start by writing down, on paper or a whiteboard, a problem that your market encounters. Then, throw out everything you can think of that goes along with that problem. Now, organize those issues into categories, and voilà! Now you have a topic with separate sections. Take that information, and find some facts and related images.

Connecting your topic to an unrelated—but more popular—topic takes a bit more creativity, but it can be worthwhile. A good example of this method would be an infographic about why someone should hire an estate planning attorney, connected to the plot of the *Hunger Games* movie *Catching Fire*.

You may not have any personal interest in the *Hunger Games*, but the fact is that the movie has been a huge success and that many of your prospects are interested in the story.

How could these seemingly unrelated topics be connected? Consider the following:

Having an estate plan and the help of an estate planning attorney is important because sometimes life throws you curveballs and the government changes the rules. You want to plan for the future. (The main character represents the client, you are the mentor, and the government remains the government.)

You can see that there are opportunities to create a storyline with your infographic. This may seem like a stretch, but if you can effectively connect your topic with something popular (like the *Hunger Games* movie), your infographic could be widely read and shared. Ultimately, that can lead to more traffic, better ranking, increased market penetration, and a good boost to your social media efforts.

Posting Your Infographics

Pinterest is a great place to post your infographics because the site is visually based. Hosting the infographic with a link to your website on your Pinterest board, and then sharing that image with your Facebook and Twitter followers, can lead to a nice increase in website traffic.

To bolster the effectiveness of your Pinterest efforts, you should "pin" the image from your blog. There should also be supporting information on your blog talking about the important issues you discuss in your infographic.

You can also email out your infographic to all the people on your email list. Instead of a newsletter, replace one month's correspondence with your new infographic. It will be a refreshing way for them to gain insights and knowledge from you.

- Infographics are some of the most shareable pieces of content on the market today.

- To make an infographic, take a topic, break it down into bite-size factoids, and create a graphic representing the facts with numbers, descriptions, and pictures.

- A useful online tool to help create infographics once you have the content is the website Piktochart (**http://piktochart.com/**).

- Connect your topic to an unrelated, popular topic. This requires some creativity but will result in an infographic that is widely read and shared, thus increasing traffic, ranking, and market penetration.

- Pinterest is a great place to post your infographics, as it's a visually-based social media platform.

PRACTICE
MANAGEMENT

SECTION 4:
PRACTICE MANAGEMENT

PROSPECTS

LINKEDIN   REFERRAL   WEBSITE   MEDIA

CLIENTS   CLIENTS   CLIENTS   CLIENTS

DOCUMENT MANAGEMENT
PAGE 289

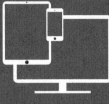

MANAGING YOUR CASES

CLIENT

WITNESS

EXPERT

AGENT

LAWYER

ADVISOR

PARALEGAL

BILLING

CASE
MANAGEMENT

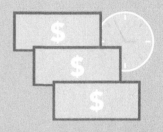

MARKETING TRENDS IN 2015

AVVO
WILL BECOME
#1 LEGAL
DIRECTORY
LISTING

IMAGES

WILL
DOMINATE

MOBILE WEBSITE DESIGN
BECOMES PRIORITY

Chapter 13:

Managing New Leads and Your Online Profile

Managing New Leads

"I Need a Plumber. . ."

Have you ever needed to hire a professional to fix a leaky drain, replace a furnace, or add an electrical circuit?

If so, how did you go about finding and hiring that person?

Maybe you had a personal referral. If so, you probably went a little more out of your way to contact the referral and waited a little bit longer for a response. But consider the far more common path, particularly when it comes to urgent issues: calling around to a series of potentially good choices until we get someone who can fix our problem.

Now think about what happens when we make these calls. What do we do when we get voicemail or no answer at all? Odds are, we simply move on to the next name on the list. The first person we end up talking to is likely to be the one who gets the job—or at a minimum, strong consideration.

Notice any similarities to your law practice? If you have a consumer-facing practice and think that your potential clients don't engage in *exactly this type of behavior*, I've got news for you: you are almost certainly wrong.

Fixing Those Leaky Legal Drains

Here's a news flash: practicing law is a service business, just like home repair contracting. And just as with home repair contractors, potential clients are calling your law office because they have a problem they need your help to solve. Clogged drainpipe, rotted floor, contested divorce—these are all issues that consumers need help with. The fact is that there are many specialized professionals willing and able to help them.

Consumers who have a problem with a leak are going to keep going down their list of plumbers until they get one that responds to them. Do you really think your potential clients are not going to call your competitor down the street if they can't get a hold of you?

The Value of Being Referred

It is true that people who are personally referred to your business will typically wait a little longer before calling someone else.

Or they may not, depending on their level of patience and the urgency of the matter.

Timely follow-up is crucial. There's a reason that the tradespeople working in your home will *always* answer the phone, even when they are laboring under your kitchen sink. They know that each of those phone calls is a potential new client. If that call goes unanswered, odds are that the caller isn't going to leave a message and passively wait for a ring back. They're simply going to call the next name on their list. Thus, it's critical to any tradesperson's business that they minimize the time it takes to follow up with a potential client.

Now ask yourself: Do you have a system in place to respond to your calls as fast as possible?

Time Is of the Essence

This real-time response needn't be limited to the phone. In the past several years, researchers have looked into the effectiveness of various response times when making contact with potential clients who make online inquiries (typically through a "lead capture" contact form).

The results illustrate, in stark terms, the benefits of immediately following up with inquiries. In auditing the results that companies experienced, researchers found a very strong correlation between the speed of the response to online inquiries and the business making contact with the potential client.

How strong of a correlation? Those who responded within one hour of the inquiry were *seven times* more likely to make contact than those who waited two hours to respond. Seven times more likely? On the difference of a single hour? This provides powerful support for the notion that consumers are moving down their list, hoping to find someone who can help them with their problem.

When compared to those who waited more than a day to get back to potential client inquiries, the within-one-hour responders were *sixty times* more likely to make contact.

It gets even worse for those who procrastinate when responding to messages.

We know that responding in one hour is seven times more effective than responding in two hours. And as it turns out, the lion's share of the value in that response is situated in the first *5 minutes* of that hour. Those responding within this golden window were four times more likely to make contact than those waiting a mere 10 minutes—and twenty-one times more likely than those hapless souls who decided to finish lunch first and respond in 30 minutes. In fact, virtually all of the opportunity to make contact occurs within the first *16 minutes* after the potential client reaches out.

It's certainly possible to make contact later than that. You might respond a week later and turn that inquiry into a client. But the data shows that your chances of doing so start to diminish as soon as the clock starts ticking—to nearly nothing within a quarter hour of a message being left.

Read more detail about these studies online[12].

Persistence

A factor in successful lead conversion that is related to immediate contact is persistent follow-up. This doesn't mean a constant barrage of phone calls but instead, perhaps, more than one. Too many attorneys assume that if a potential client doesn't respond to a single return message, then the potential client really isn't interested. Most sales professionals will tell you that it typically takes multiple return calls—often between four and seven—in order to make contact.

This is all the more reason to answer the phone the first time and respond to messages immediately.

---

12   http://hbr.org/2011/03/the-short-life-of-online-sales-leads/ar/1
        http://www.leadresponsemanagement.org/lrm_study

The Value of Process

So what's the takeaway for attorneys? It's simple, really: those who serve consumers should emulate tradespeople and immediately follow up on inquiries from potential clients. With nearly all successful follow-up being made within minutes of an inquiry coming in, the impact of consistently speedy responses cannot be understated.

This is particularly true for attorneys who are paying for lead generation. Attorneys pay more per lead than virtually any other service provider. There is the potential for orders-of-magnitude improvement in business development just by implementing the mindset and systems to immediately respond to leads.

What kind of system? Think of it as a mixture of rules and tools. The rules are business processes established and monitored to ensure that phones are covered, calls are answered, and online/email/chat inquiries get an immediate response. The tools can be as simple as an Excel spreadsheet tracking inbound inquiries or as sophisticated as a powerful Customer Relationship Management (CRM) system such as Salesforce or Avvo Ignite.

Take some time to determine what the rules should be for your practice. This may include staff training, or it may be simply adjusting your own mindset to immediately address new client inquiries. For the tools, evaluate your CRM options (you can get a free trial of Avvo Ignite), but don't wait to track your inquiries: use whatever tools—even pen and paper, if necessary—that you are comfortable with. Make sure that you are following up diligently, quickly, and more than once.

The Long-Term Benefits

Having a good system for follow-up and customer management can also yield big benefits when calculating the effectiveness of your marketing channels. Used diligently over a matter of months, such a system will tell your firm where each inquiry originates (e.g. the firm's website, a search marketing campaign, the yellow pages, etc.).

Over time, your firm will then be able to tell the rate at which inquiries from each marketing channel turn into actual clients. This may show, for example, that while a billboard ad is driving a lot of calls, such contacts become clients at a far lower rate than the much smaller number of potential clients generated from a local newsletter campaign. By layering the cost of these marketing initiatives on the number of clients generated, your firm can get a very clear picture of the return on investment of each initiative (i.e. what it costs to generate a client). That information allows your firm to identify those channels where it can profitably increase its marketing investment—and those that it needs to scale back or discontinue.

Managing Your Online Profile

As word of mouth moves online, lawyers are in the same place today that hotels were a decade ago: just starting to face the widespread use of online user reviews and worried that such reviews will sabotage their businesses. Hotels—like restaurants and the consumer products before them—have learned to live with, and quite often leverage, the phenomenon of online reviews. While no system of reviews is perfect, getting enough liquidity into the "reputational ecosystem" has created a resource that helps expose those providers offering subpar service and celebrate the virtues of those that shine.

Lawyers would be wise to recognize the inevitability of this trend in professional services. Unfortunately, we are too often hyper-focused on the potential for negative and phony reviews, which can cause paralysis and failure to adapt to this massive change in how clients are researching lawyers.

Reviews Are Important

According to the latest Nielsen survey data, consumer reviews posted online are now the second-most trusted source of marketing information for consumers. Trailing only "recommendations from people known" (i.e. the gold standard of personal referrals), online reviews now rank ahead of websites and editorial content—and far ahead of traditional paid advertising media. Consumers are also increasingly expecting to get this type of information when making local purchasing decisions.

Yes, You Will Get a Negative Review

As the number of online reviews grow, one thing is near-certain: every attorney—even the most attentive, empathetic, and outstanding in our ranks—will receive a negative review someday. There are many reasons for this, but the two most important are that clients are unpredictable and may have unreasonable expectations and that no open reputational ecosystem can be completely free of inaccurate or hyperbolic feedback. Over time, and with sufficient liquidity, the overall tenor of the reviews for a business will paint an accurate picture. But any given review may widely miss the mark—in either direction. Or it may be phony. Accept these imperfections (they are never going to be completely eliminated), and focus on managing your online reputation.

Handling the Negative

- **Think twice (or better yet, three times) before suing.** For many lawyers, the first instinct when facing something negative online is to threaten to bring a defamation lawsuit. But this is almost always a bad idea, for three reasons: You can't sue the identifiable and likely deeper-pocketed forum provider, as they are immune from defamation liability for publishing third party comments under 47 USC 230. If you haven't pled a solid case, you may be on the hook for the defendant's attorneys fees under state anti-SLAPP law. And due to what's known as the "Streisand Effect," making a fuss about something you don't like online can easily result in the negative content getting exponentially more attention than it would have otherwise received.

- **Consider whether you earned it.** Gut-wrenching as it may be, staying objective in the face of negative feedback is critical. Online feedback is free research into how your practice is perceived by clients. If you get a negative review, the very first thing to consider is whether there may be some truth to it. Perhaps there is a blind spot in your practice or even a staff person who, out of your sight, is treating your clients contemptuously. In the past, you would never have an opportunity to learn of this kind of client frustration. Embrace the window into your practice that regular online feedback can give you.

- **Keep the big picture in mind.** Consider a typical consumer reaction to a hotel or restaurant with nothing but unalloyed, glowing comments. You might think the reviews could be fake, right? No product or service, no matter how wonderful, pleases everyone. Consumers expect that any credible site with more than a handful of reviews will include a smattering of neutral to negative feedback. And consumers are getting increasingly savvy about online feedback. They are hungry for detail and generally dismissive of broad generalizations and hyperbole, good or bad. If you've gotten a dozen or more comments that are 100 percent positive, a negative review or two might actually do you some good by making your positive reviews more credible.

- **Leave a comment.** Negative commentary can actually be an excellent marketing opportunity. By posting a professional, meaningful response to negative commentary, you send a powerful message to any readers of that review. Done correctly, such a message communicates responsiveness, attention to feedback, and strength of character. The trick is to not get defensive or petty or feel the need to directly refute what you perceive is wrong with the review. It's far more effective to think of future readers, rather than the original reviewer, when writing the comment. Think of what they'd want to hear—that you care about feedback even after you've been paid, that you want to make things right for your customers, that you have compassion for their situations—and invest adequate time and attention in crafting an effective message. Remember that a poorly handled response to a negative review is much worse than no response at all, as it makes you look thin-skinned and defensive. Worse yet, if you are argumentative and reveal client confidences (or even potentially harmful non-confidences) in your comment, you may be subject to bar discipline.

- **Do not succumb to the temptation of "astroturfing."** Online review platforms are fairly open. While there is a nascent movement to tie reviews directly to a purchase (such as Amazon's verified purchaser reviews), most sites require relatively little information from a reviewer in order to post. So it may be tempting to leave positive reviews for yourself or pay others to do so for you. There's a name for this practice: astroturfing. This is false advertising, which will easily lead to bar discipline (and significant public shaming) for any attorney caught doing it. Several dozen businesses and marketing agencies have been prosecuted by the New York Attorney General's office for astroturfing, paying hundreds of thousands of dollars in fines in the process. Earn your positive reviews. Don't generate fake ones.

- **Turn negative feedback into your marketing message.** This can be a hard one to get right, and it certainly won't work for everyone. But confident attorneys—particularly those with successful niche practices—can actually use negative feedback as a marketing message. By bringing attention to a negative review that's based on unreasonable expectations (or is simply hyperbolic or incoherent), your firm can communicate a message that hits several areas: confidence, exclusivity, and a certain edginess. It also sends a message about the inherent unreliability of any single piece of consumer feedback. A number of restaurants have done this successfully: servers at San Francisco's Delfina Pizza all wear shirts imprinted with one-star reviews the restaurant has received on Yelp. If you've got the right kind of practice and enough confidence, maybe the next negative review can be part of your marketing message.

Inoculate Your Practice against Negative Reviews

- **Ask for reviews.** Smart businesses realize that the surest way to lessen the impact of a negative review—and to maximize the free market research aspect of online reviews—is to ensure that they get a wealth of regular feedback from clients. So they make it a practice to regularly ask for reviews. From post-purchase emails, to survey instructions on the bottom of receipts, to cards handed out in a medical clinic waiting room, sellers of goods and services in virtually all industries are proactively seeking input from users. While it may feel strange to ask, it's worth it to make requesting feedback part of your file-closing procedure. Avvo and other sites have tools to make it easy to do so. And lest you think that only the cranks want to leave feedback, it's actually the opposite that is true: happy customers are more likely to leave feedback. This is particularly true where the services are high cost or high stress—and law fits both of those parameters. In fact, at Avvo, attorney reviews have consistently run better than 80 percent positive.

- **Build a wall of content.** There is an old advertising adage that says, when it comes to expensive purchases, "Long copy sells." It's a concept that goes back to *Mad Men* days, but it remains true today: someone who is prepared to spend serious money wants as much information as possible. Such purchasers are far less likely to respond to buzzwords or taglines. Adding to this tendency are the rapid growth of consumer reviews and the increasing suspicion of products and services that are not reviewed. The legal services market hasn't quite hit this point yet, but it's coming. Consider your own behavior when researching products on Amazon, hotels on TripAdvisor, or restaurants on Yelp. What does an absence of reviews make you think? Building a wall of content—through enhancing your Avvo profile, soliciting reviews regularly, writing blog posts and articles, etc.—ensures that any potential client researching your services will have that long copy. The wealth of information will help potential clients get comfortable with their decision to retain you and will also offset the inevitable negative review.

About Avvo

Avvo.com is the web's largest legal Q&A forum, directory, and legal marketplace (http://www.avvo.com). Avvo's features and benefits include:

- Profiles and ratings for nearly every attorney in the United States, based on public licensing, disciplinary, and biographical data

- A separate rating for each attorney based on client feedback

- More than five million monthly visitors, which drives hundreds of thousands of contacts to attorneys each month

- A free Q&A forum featuring thousands of questions from consumers every week

- Avvo Ignite Suite, Avvo's simple-to-use lead management platform that allows attorneys and law office staff to track and follow up with potential clients faster and more effectively than ever before, all while tracking the effectiveness of the firm's marketing spend

Founded in 2007 in Seattle, Avvo is privately held with funding from Benchmark Capital, Ignition Partners, and DAG Ventures.

Chapter 14:

Keeping Up with Jones & Jones LLC: Effective Practice Management for a Successful Law Firm

As most legal professionals are painfully aware, running a law practice is hard work—and private practice is increasingly the reality for the modern law grad. Unfortunately, legal aptitude is rarely a proxy for business acumen, and many would agree that the current system of legal education is doing a poor job of arming graduates with the entrepreneurial skills and organizational tools required to operate a successful practice. Despite this, legal professionals are held to an incredibly high standard of operational competence, where the dire penalties for failure can result in a breach of ethics, malpractice, and even disbarment. This is a problem that has been challenging the alignment of legal professionals and their respective regulators for decades. It is a problem that practice management tools such as Clio set out to remedy.

In 2007, while working as contractors to the Law Society of British Columbia (LSBC), the founders of Clio, Rian Gauvreau and Jack Newton, learned of an LSBC study that evaluated the cause of malpractice and competence-related infractions among their solo and small firm membership. The study found three areas of failure that occurred considerably more frequently among small firms, when compared to their larger firm counterparts. These three core, but preventable, areas were missed limitations dates, insufficient or incorrect trust accounting, and poor client communication. Ironically, software systems have been available for years that help to address these sources of concern; however, the LSBC discovered that, despite their availability, adoption of these software solutions were remarkably low among small firms. For many, the high cost of maintenance and acquisition, coupled with the complex learning curve and technical overhead, created a daunting barrier to adoption. It was this discovery that served as the catalyst for the creation of Clio and, ultimately, a practice management solution that alleviated the common barriers to adoption while supporting the dynamic practice demands of the modern legal professional.

Since 2008, at Clio, we've had a front-row seat to many rapid technological changes in the legal industry. The rise of the smartphone, the advent of the tablet, and the prevalence of cloud-based applications are challenging legal professionals from all walks to embrace technology as an essential part of succeeding in modern practice. Like never before, lawyers using cloud-based applications such as Clio, Google Apps, and Dropbox can work with unfettered mobility and accessibility—all with unprecedented affordability, cost predictability, security, and redundancy. These tools are also helping to level the playing field between small and large firm attorneys. Best-in-class technology is no longer exclusively available to the AMLAW 500; the Cloud and new web-based tools have helped to democratize the information technology landscape and are enabling small to mid-sized firms to compete effectively in a rapidly changing legal market.

Saving Time with Cloud-Based Tools

Beyond the competitive benefits, cloud-based tools are also helping lawyers to improve efficiency and, in many cases, better work-life balance. It's no secret that lawyers score among those professionals with the lowest average levels of job satisfaction. A recent internal survey of our users asked, on average, how many hours per day practice management software was able to save them in terms of improved workflow and efficiency. The answer was an astonishing 1.7 hours per day, which equates to 8.5 hours per week: time that most acknowledged was a major contributor to a greater sense of freedom and overall happiness. Moreover, much of this saved time allowed firms to focus more time on client care and effective communication, which helps not only to satisfy an ethical responsibility but also to reinforce value and develop a reputable brand.

A simple example of time-saving opportunities would be to put your top 10, or most used, activity descriptions at the top of your daily to-do list on your SaaS (Software as a Service)-based practice management notification tool.

Meeting Client Expectations

In an increasingly saturated and rarely differentiated market, brand and client experience are factors that firms cannot afford to overlook. In addition to being a powerful organizational tool, a cloud-based practice management system can help to facilitate an exceptional client experience via case visibility, collaboration, and communication. Integrated features, such as a client collaboration portal, afford clients unprecedented access to key case updates and information, and they provide a medium for the easy exchange of messages, documents, appointments, tasks and invoices. In addition to assisting lawyers in their duty to provide regular communication, collaborative tools have also been shown to help firms improve their billable recovery rates. This is in part due to an improved client experience but is also thanks to available integrations such as LawPay and ZenCash, which respectively allow firms to collect payments online via credit card and allow for outsourced recovery management.

Keeping Up with Billing

Recovery, however, inevitably depends on a system that reliably and dynamically captures time and expenses and streamlines the billable process. A recent article by Bruce MacEwen and Janet Stanton in the *Association of Legal Administrators* magazine, titled "Billable Hours: Under-Reported and Killing Your Firm's Bottom Line,"[13] revealed some stark discoveries about under-reported recoverables and how these are conspiring to harm the viability of many firms. The article found that among those surveyed, up to 30 percent of legitimate billables were not being effectively captured, leading to an average of between $20,000 and $40,000 of lost billing opportunity. Given that many firms are struggling to operate under heavy competitive pressure and thin margins, a seamlessly integrated time-capture and billing system such as Clio is designed to maximize firm profitability by plugging the opportunities for time leakage. Mobile and desktop time capture, expense management, and integrated activity monitoring tools ensure that attorneys and other legal professionals are not necessarily spending more time working; rather, they're just being properly compensated for the hard work already invested on behalf of their clients. Additionally, many firms without a formal practice management or timekeeping system are burdened with the agonizing and time-consuming process of monthly time collation and bill generation. Practice management systems further help to optimize firm efficiency by streamlining and automating

---

13   http://www.smart-webparts.com/pdfs/lawfirmsurvey.pdf

the bill generation process. For most firms, this can result in a monthly savings of more than three hours per attorney.

Unfortunately, time capture and billing is, in some cases, not enough to ensure firm success. Costly practice areas, highly competitive environments, weak contributors, and deadbeat clients can all act as invisible, deadly forces that work in opposition to firm viability. Simply logging time and issuing regular bills may be sufficient for some, but many other firms find themselves puzzled by the inability to maintain solvency despite a diligent billing workflow. In such cases, tools for more in-depth business insight can help to identify the underlying flaws that, if corrected, can foster firm success. Firm reports are so crucial that, at Clio, we work to provide visibility into such metrics, including recovery rates, billable contributions, work in progress, and practice area profitability—all of which can help attorneys and staff monitor and adapt to the changing health of the organization. Also, a practice management tool that offers integrated trust reporting and accounting can aid in the management of IOTA/IOLTA trust transactions, ensuring a detailed audit record and a reliable method for attributing client holdings in a pooled account. This can also help to satisfy regulatory trust record and reporting requirements and work to prevent one of the more frequent sources of attorney error and discipline.

Client Security

In addition to helping promote firm financial security, cloud-based systems also ensure client security through organization and redundancy. Juggling the needs and individual requirements of multiple clients can be incredibly challenging and can expose both the client and the attorney to considerable risk in the event that a critical task or event is missed. If for no other reason, an effective practice management solution, like Clio, should help attorneys protect their clients' interests by minimizing (or eliminating) the likelihood of organizational failure. Integrated calendaring, task management, timelines, notes, and alerts all serve the interests of both parties and protect against the kinds of oversight that can lead to competence-related concerns as identified by the LSBC. Also, having been proven as an effective preventative measure against attorney oversight, use of a practice management solution will often reduce the risk to malpractice carriers, resulting in significant savings on insurance premiums.

Since the widespread adoption of digital tools in modern practice, risk has also manifested in the form of data confidentiality and redundancy. Traditional client-server systems have always required a level of care and maintenance that, if not performed, could expose client data to loss or breach of confidentiality. Nevertheless, until the availability of cloud solutions, firms were forced to keep up their technological housekeeping at the cost of their time and money, or at the expense of their duty to their clients. This problem has now, in part, been alleviated by virtue of the safeguards and redundancies that are standard practice among most cloud-based software providers in the legal market. While additional redundancy and security protections are never a bad idea, firms can now rest assured that their client information is subject to industry-leading redundancy and security measures that far exceed what a typical firm could provide for themselves. This also includes such measures as encrypted data transmission, geographic redundancy, and service level guarantees that surpass what could normally be expected from traditional client-server-based products.

Avoid Making Major Ethical Mistakes

Despite the general expectation of greater redundancy and security, selection of any software system (whether cloud-based or not) should still be met with the rigor of some due diligence. Simply placing implicit trust in a software provider is never wise, and it's always a good idea to look into the guarantees and safeguards that the provider is extending to the firm and the customer. Most often, these commitments are outlined in the form of a terms of service document, but these may also include a privacy policy and service level agreement (SLA). Alone or in conjunction, these documents should define the terms of ownership, usage provisions, software availability, redundancy measures, location of storage, liability, payment terms, and cancellation policy. Although many state bars and attorney regulators have acknowledged that reasonable care is a sufficient diligence standard to ensure client confidentiality, firms should exercise proper care when selecting a provider and seek guidance from their local bar practice management advisor when in doubt.

Ultimately, a practice management system of any kind is a valuable investment in firm success; however, the rise of cloud-based software means that world-class, turn-key tools such as Clio, Google Apps, and Dropbox are available affordably, with negligible implementation or maintenance overhead. Firms can operate, compete, and collaborate virtually—from any device, at any location—while ensuring the health of their practice through integrated time capture, billing, and reporting tools. This can provide an unprecedented client experience, underpinned by visibility, communication, and confidentiality.

This thesis, along with legions of highly engaged users and valued advocates, is what has helped Clio grow, from its humble beginnings in 2008, to the leading and most widely used provider of web-based practice management in the legal industry. Clio is now offered as a member benefit with more than 30 state and local bar associations and is in use in over one hundred top law schools, paralegal programs, and legal clinics, along with many public sector organizations, government agencies, and NGOs. Clio as a platform has also integrated with many of the legal industry's leading providers, including Google, Dropbox, Box, NetDocuments, LawPay, DirectLaw, Chrometa, ZenCash, and RightSignature, among many others.

About Clio

Founded in 2007, Clio was produced with the cooperation and advice of bar associations and law societies across North America, with the goal of creating an easy-to-use, intuitive, web-based practice management system. Clio's core functionality delivers the tools that small to mid-sized firms need to run their practice: calendaring, time tracking, note-taking, document management, trust accounting, retainer management, and time recording and billing.

Clio's SaaS-based practice management tools are ideally suited for solicitors, barristers, and legal professionals that want to improve efficiencies within their practice and external collaboration. The company is headquartered in Vancouver, Canada and has staff operating in Canada and Ireland. Clio is a trademark of Themis Solutions, Inc.

Readers of this book can apply the code "GNGF" to receive 25 percent off of their first six months of Clio. Learn more about Clio and sign up for your free trial at www.goclio.com.

Chapter 15:

Document Management in a Hybrid Paper-Digital World

It's no secret that the legal industry produces a lot of paper and will do so for the foreseeable future. For all the talk about the "paperless office," the reality is that the legal profession, like so many other industries, will use paper documents for many years to come. That said, countless firms are looking for ways to incorporate digital documents and electronic processes into their practices to increase efficiency and support web-based activities.

If you're thinking about or already transitioning to a more digital environment, you need to think about the tools and processes that will help you make the most of your digital information.

First Step: Scanning Your Paper Documents

The first step is digitizing your paper-based information. For years, many solo lawyers and small firms have avoided purchasing dedicated scanning devices due to their cost and potential complexity. Many smaller firms resort to multi-function machines—devices that scan, print, copy, and fax—in order to save on hardware costs. At larger firms, a common approach involves placing high-performance, dedicated scanners in central areas, requiring lawyers and other employees to leave their desks to perform scanning tasks; however, there are now better alternatives on the market.

Today's scanning technology is incredibly sophisticated, affordable, and compact, giving attorneys cost-effective and powerful tools that allow them to digitize paper documents right on their desks. There's no compromise to functionality and durability and no need to waste valuable time walking to another room. Small desktop scanners with small area footprints can now scan 20 to 30 pages or more per minute, provide duplexing functionality (capturing both sides of a sheet in one pass), and offer intuitive menus for saving scanned documents to specific locations and even cloud services.

Be sure to look for devices that come with essential software packages, such as Adobe Acrobat and optical character recognition (OCR), for creating quick, searchable PDF files from paper documents.

Once you've settled on scanning technology, it's time to consider how you are going to organize your digital content. Let's take a high-level look at some best-practice document management concepts for law firms.

Clients, Matters, and a Document Management System for Lawyers

Law firms of all sizes usually manage files by focusing on two things:

1) The client

2) The matter that's being handled

In the common parlance of law office administrators and law firm consultants, the phrase most commonly heard is "matter-centric." In other words, lawyers typically organize their cases by matter.

Matters are grouped together based on the client. It is necessary to pay close attention to the client because ethics dictate that lawyers can't work for a client if there is a conflict of interest. When you take on a new case, you'll need to define whom you are representing. You'll have to keep tabs on the client during the representation—and possibly for several years after the representation is over.

Clients who come to a lawyer for one matter will often wind up hiring the lawyer to handle others. As a result, lawyers will continue to organize their case information by client and matter.

So how does this affect your document management?

For a number of years, large law firms have purchased and used document management systems, commonly known by the acronym "DMS." In the world of digital information management, a DMS is sometimes viewed as the equivalent of a folder in a filing cabinet stored in a document repository, which is a flawed analogy.

A DMS can do a lot more than simply store documents: it can also help quickly organize documents in a logical fashion, offer tools for rapid access, and provide ways of safely securing them for long periods.

A DMS can be configured to suit the needs of many different kinds of businesses. For your law firm, the DMS can be arranged according to the client-matter hierarchy that is fundamental to the legal industry. Your digital files can be organized by matter and grouped by client.

HERE ARE TWO EXAMPLES:

Tom Smith - Client 0001

Entertainment contract - Matter 0001

Divorce from first wife - Matter 0002

Franchise business - Matter 0003

Frank Jones - Client 0002

FJI contracting incorporation documents - Matter 0001

Fabricamp lawsuit - Matter 0002

The client-matter number for Tom Smith's divorce would be 0001-0002. The client-matter number for Frank Jones' incorporation is 0002-0001.

This kind of numbering system is easy to set up in a DMS. It's easier than writing names, and it helps ensure the confidentiality of the lawyers' client information.

Moreover, with an effective DMS, you can search for, filter, and access client and matter information much faster and more efficiently than you can with paper-based files.

Using the Cloud for a Simple DMS

In the past, having a DMS meant owning and operating your own server. This would often present significant cost and operational barriers to adoption by smaller firms. They couldn't afford to buy a server-based DMS or the ongoing IT work needed to maintain it.

However, with the proliferation of cloud-based services—such as SugarSync, Dropbox, and Google Drive—it's now possible for lawyers to use a cloud solution for a basic DMS. This is more affordable and minimizes IT issues, as the hardware and ongoing maintenance is provided as part of the subscription cost of each service. For starting costs of about $100 annually, your firm can establish a cost-effective way to store and access documents—and can access them virtually anywhere and from a wide range of devices.

What Problems Does a DMS Solve?

These consumer-level cloud services are inherently very basic. They often lack strong security features, and they typically rely on nested folder structures that can be inadequate for firms as they grow in size—and as their document management needs develop.

That's when it's time to consider more sophisticated document management services like NetDocuments. These services can help with issues such as:

- Locating misfiled documents

- Recovering inadvertently deleted documents

- Establishing who can access specific documents—either by individual user or category of user–and monitoring who has been accessing documents

- Automatically notifying users of the arrival of a new document if it's relevant to a matter they're working on

- Managing emails related to a specific client or matter

- Managing different versions of documents (version control)

- Accessing documents remotely

Historically, only lawyers in large law firms could afford systems that provided features like these; however, dropping costs have provided an entry point for solo lawyers and small firms that want to take advantage of the same business functionality enjoyed by larger organizations.

Key Functions of a DMS

Let's look a bit more closely into the core functions a DMS will provide to your law firm.

Save Function

The first thing a DMS should do is take over the save function of every software application used by the firm.

Ideally, a DMS will integrate with every type of software application, especially those that are used to create or edit documents, such as Microsoft Office applications. Once the DMS is installed, a lawyer or secretary who is saving a document will be forced to save it through the DMS. The DMS then decides where to store the documents. Gone are the days of navigating through a series of nested folders on a shared network drive.

The only choices for users to make—and these are important choices that will require some training—include selecting a document name, which should conform to established naming conventions, and the type of document, such as correspondence, pleading, or legal research. The user will also have to fill in a field with the client number and/or matter number as well as the client's full name. These fields can be set up just once, and then it's easy to automate the process of profiling documents without a lot of typing.

A good DMS can also help with the proliferation of email used in legal work. While Microsoft Exchange allows users to set up shared folders, it lacks reliable tools for notifying users working on common matters that a new email has been added to the DMS. A DMS solution enables users to easily add emails that are related to a client matter simply by dragging them into the DMS. In fact, it's the ability of a modern DMS to manage email that makes it indispensable for today's law firm.

Store Function

In addition to the save function, a DMS needs to be configured with storage goals in mind. Where the storage is located will depend on what kind of DMS you use.

A server-based DMS will store documents locally on a computer server that your law firm controls and manages. Today, document management systems also offer cloud-based functionality that allows documents to be stored on servers hosted by third parties, with document access provided over the Internet from any location. This also allows a DMS to be configured for reliable off-site backup.

Filter & Search Function

Along with the save and store functions, a DMS lets you find documents quickly. How documents are found depends to some extent on the fields that were created to profile the documents.

There are two basic ways to retrieve documents from a DMS:

Filtering based on key field(s), such as matter, client, type of document, or date range for creation or modification of the document

Searching for text within the document, assuming the document has text that is searchable (which underscores the importance of having "searchable PDF" functionality in place when scanning paper documents)

Law practices are inundated with documents, so being able to find information by filtering and searching text is crucial. This is another reason why a DMS trumps simple nested folders.

Searching for crucial data that's simply stored on a network drive can be a slow, frustrating process that quickly reveals the shortcomings of using nested folders. You might be able to limp along with this approach if you are a solo practitioner. But in a firm with more than one lawyer, the addition of each new user adds an exponential level of potential chaos to the process of finding documents—or recovering documents that are inadvertently lost.

Collaboration Function

Finally, there is a function of a DMS that is often overlooked or underused: support for collaboration. A good DMS helps lawyers and legal professionals collaborate better than they would in a paper-based world or in a digital document system built around basic cloud services.

We mentioned earlier that lawyers can store case-related emails in a DMS. But a DMS makes collaboration possible for *any* kind of document that it manages, not just emails. A DMS can notify any lawyer working on a client matter that a new pleading has been added, making it easy to quickly review that pleading.

Equally important, shared access to such documents will not cause the document to become corrupted, nor will it lead to versioning conflicts, as is often the case when using basic cloud services or local, nested-structure file systems.

What's the Next Step?

If you are looking to get away from paper and bring your practice into the digital age, you should begin by investing in reliable, dedicated scanning hardware. Then you should evaluate document management systems, which are the best and most reliable means of managing digital documents. The hardware and software technology available today is not just economical and easy to use—it's becoming essential for practice management in a digital world.

Fujitsu Computer Products of America

Fujitsu Computer Products of America is responsible for distribution, sales and marketing, finance and administration, and engineering and technical support for the Fujitsu document imaging scanner business in the United States. The company provides the strength, backing, and resources of one of the world's largest computer companies.

Fujitsu's Imaging Products Group (IPG) is an established leader in the Document Imaging Market, featuring innovative scanning solutions and services in the personal, workgroup, departmental, and production-level scanner categories. Fujitsu's revolutionary scanners, including the ScanSnap scanners, "fi Series" workgroup scanners, and "fi Series" department scanners, provide customers with a broad range of scanning options that deliver speed, image quality, paper handling, and ease of integration and compatibility with other imaging applications.

Fujitsu Computer Products of America Inc.'s experience in its product areas, strong relationships with U.S. resellers and software partners, advanced research and development into the industry's latest technologies, and keen awareness of customer needs have all contributed to its continued success.

For more information about Fujitsu products and services, call us at 800-626-4686 or 408-746-7000.

For additional information, visit: http://www.fcpa.fujitsu.com.

Ernest Svenson

Ernest Svenson spent two years working as a law clerk to a federal trial judge and then practiced commercial litigation for 26 years—the last six years as a solo practitioner. He started his weblog *Ernie the Attorney* in 2002, and shortly after that, it was chosen by the ABA Journal as one of the top 100 law weblogs. He has started several other blogs, including PDFforLawyers.com, which is about using PDFs in the practice of law. He has two books published by the ABA, *Blogging in One Hour for Lawyers* and his soon-to-be-released book *Acrobat in One Hour for Lawyers*.

Ernie lives in Louisiana, where he puts on CLE seminars about technology in law and online webinars at the site PaperlessChase.com. He believes that the practice of law is largely an "information processing business," and his goal is to help lawyers find more efficient ways to process their information.

Ernie enjoys photography, golf, and music. He likes to play his guitar for captive audiences, who quickly escape once he starts singing.

Ernie's contact info:

504-613-4253 (main)

504-202-0688 (cell)

ernie@paperlesschase.com

Adriana Linares

Adriana Linares is a legal technology trainer and consultant with LawTech Partners, a professional services firm specializing in the legal industry. The firm's services include legal technology consulting and law office software training. Using her practical and personal approach to learning, she helps legal professionals maximize their technology skills and investments.

Having spent her formidable career years at two of Florida's largest law firms, Adriana went on to open LawTech Partners in 2004. She has recently launched Help Desk for Lawyers—a remote training and support service focused on solo and small firms. She is a frequent speaker at national technology conferences and a regular contributor to legal blogs and publications. She spent four years on the Planning Board of the ABA TECHSHOW and two years as an editor for Technolawyer's Blawgworld. In 2013, she was named one of the Fastcase Top 50 Global Legal Innovators.

Today, she serves as a technology consultant to the Florida Bar Communications Committee. She is chair of the Research & Technology Subcommittee of the Law Practice Division of the ABA, and serves on the advisory board for the Center for Law Practice Technology. She also eagerly chairs the Technology Section of the Osceola County Bar, overseeing their No Attorney Left Behind initiative—a technology competence training program. Adriana has a Bachelor of Science Degree in Geography from Stetson

University and a Master of Arts Degree in Corporate Communication and Technology from Rollins. She speaks fluent Spanish.

Adriana Linares

LawTech Partners

www.lawtechpartners.com

training@lawtechpartners.com

407-409-8828

Chapter 16:

Marketing Trends in 2015

In our past few books, we have avoided talking about predictions and trying to peer into the impossibly murky crystal ball that is the Internet's future. Well, just like search engines, this time we are changing things up a bit. Here is our best take on what 2015 could have in store for marketing your law firm.

Mobile Applications for Law Firms

Not that law firm mobile applications were popular to begin with, but we predict they will be mostly obsolete in 2015. With the advent of HTML5 and the rise of better native programs for law firm websites, the need for a separate application for prospects is likely to become pointless. Unless someone is currently a client, it is difficult to find a great case for a law firm mobile app to begin with. Unless your application provides regular usefulness to the prospect or client, why would they even download it? Put your energy in developing a mobile friendly website that has all the functionality of a mobile application with the added benefit of being found in mobile search and without requiring the prospect to download anything—then you have a winning combination.

It will be possible to program mobile websites to capture and upload images from accidents, provide calculation tables for estate planning, and get access to case updates. At GNGF, we are already designing websites with mobile in mind first and working our way backwards; this is because mobile traffic to law firm websites is becoming so important.

The only exception to this will be quality mobile applications that provide a client portal for updating your clients throughout their case. These will not be custom mobile apps developed by law firms but should be provided by the vendor you will use for your practice management software.

Law Firms Fully Embrace Social Media

Up until now, most of our conversations with law firms about social media have been rather negative. From ethical concerns to flat out not caring, lawyers have tried to ignore social media until 2015. As the opinion on Model

Rule 1.1: Competence now includes technology, lawyers will have to start learning how social media functions to better advise their clients. This will have two impacts: 1) a deeper understanding of the capabilities of social media as a communication medium and 2) a broader adoption of social media marketing strategies.

As more firms begin to benefit from marketing on social media, the competition will drive other lawyers into fits of jealous rage. Soon, all law firms will see the benefits of a thoughtful social media marketing strategy. These campaigns will focus on genuine engagement, using only social networks that drive the best prospects.

Pricing Pressure Drives More Branding

With a steady flow of new graduates from law school, expansion of companies offering legal information (like LegalZoom and Access Legal), disruptors to the market (similar to Avvo's dial-an-attorney model), and savvy consumers, law firms will begin to feel the brunt of years of pricing pressure. In order to insulate themselves from this downward spiral, law firms will start to invest in improving their brand messaging. This will help law firms effectively communicate to clients the value of hiring them over their competitors or any websites offering less expensive alternatives. Because of the increase in need for proper branding, schools will start including branding for third year students...just kidding, law schools would never do that.

Images Will Dominate Marketing

Content will continue to be important, but users' attention spans will not increase. This will lead law firms to start creating better visual marketing campaigns to attract visitors. Infographics will make a comeback in the legal space. Stand-alone websites will be created to visually display solutions for individuals.

This will also put an end to traditional stock images for websites, blogs, and social posts. Instead, law firms will seek out better photography and more custom images for use in their marketing.

Like all things great in marketing, agencies will jump on this trend and completely ruin images as an effective marketing strategy by flooding the market with thousands of image-based marketing campaigns. Way to go marketers!

Hybrid LawyMarketer Position Will Be Created

Law firms will hire a lawyer, who is also a marketer, and will respect him or her. This new position will be part-time practicing lawyer and part-time marketing contributor. His or her main function will be to post on social channels, write blogs, respond to prospects online, and research creative methods for attracting more prospects.

This hybrid position will not replace marketing departments, but it will be an augmentation to the team. The lawyer/marketer (LawyMarketer) will be available to provide the crucial legal insights to the marketing department's campaigns. With their extensive legal knowledge, these individuals will be uniquely positioned to impact the effectiveness of the law firm's marketing strategy by adding the right level of lawyer-speak to the marketing material.

Wearable Technology Changes The Game

With the wide adoption of wearable technology, law firms will be able to send marketing information to individuals that may be in need of legal assistance. When someone has connected his or her wearable technology to a social network, the law firm will be able to market to individuals who meet certain psychographic conditions. For example, a law firm can market to someone who begins visiting the drug store, a physical therapist office building, and who has recently stopped playing tennis at the club. That person would, given their actions, possibly be in need of a personal injury attorney.

Ethics boards will work overtime to limit the scope of marketing that can be directed at individuals based on wearable technology. Some lawyers will decide to ignore these opinions and do it anyway, resulting in a slew of new ethics violation hearings.

The final determination will be that one cannot know why a person may decide on a certain change in behavior, thus sending marketing information to these individuals is, in fact, ethically acceptable. This will be argued at length.

Avvo Will Dominate 2015

Avvo continues to dominate the search engines while introducing game-changing ideas. LegalZoom falls asleep at the wheel as Avvo starts providing legal documents. Other directory listings become relics because users have more control within the Avvo system. Online options that include connecting with attorneys for a brief conversation lead to a great revenue source for law firms.

Google determines that Avvo is the best legal directory for searchers and decides to add consumer reviews as a ranking factor. This leaves FindLaw and Lawyers.com to be relegated to Page 2 of the search engines, also known as "virtually invisible."

Mobile Website Design Becomes Priority

With mobile use to access the Internet exceeding that of desktop, law firms will invest heavily in mobile-ready websites. Responsive design becomes the only viable option for effectively displaying your website on various-sized devices.

Many law firms will make the mistake of having a designer without any marketing knowledge create their website, thus rendering the mobile version inadequate. With over 50 percent of mobile users wanting access to phone numbers and directions, mobile websites will have to be redesigned to provide users with the information that they want in the way that they want it.

Video Conferencing and Meetings

To combat the increased pricing pressure, law firms will start offering virtual lawyers to assist with basic legal questions for some incoming clients. Some law firms will attempt to go 100 percent virtual, only to realize that it doesn't really work for building a successful practice.

With options like FaceTime, Skype, Gchat, and GoToMeeting, the ability to connect through video has finally become easy. Clients will prefer the video option to phone conversations because of the increased rapport it allows them to establish with their lawyer. Some law firms will send video cameras to remote areas as a method of securing a strong client relationship.

Practice Management Solutions Free Up Lawyer's Time

Firms will start to migrate heavily towards practice management and case management solutions. This will improve the law firm's efficiency in dealing with client matters, and it will have a positive impact on the billing process. All this will lead to time-savings for the individual lawyers within the firm. Of course, you'll just use this time to do more work.

Intake Process Becomes Integral Part of Law Firm Marketing

Understanding who, where, and how someone became a client will lead to improved marketing decisions. With the availability of cookies and tracking software, law firms will start to manage their marketing funnel with finely tuned data. This will lead to an increase in marketing efforts towards a holistic web presence. Law firms will realize that people on the Internet look at more than one source. This will also validate the need for a strong web presence to protect your referral business.

Online Law Practice Strategies: 2015 Edition Will Be a Best-Seller

Why not predict your own success?

ABOUT GNGF

In the interest of full disclosure, we also run a marketing agency for law firms. We work exclusively with clients in the legal industry, and we do it all—branding, website design, SEO, paid advertising, content creation, social media, and video—to help attorneys and law firms get more clients and grow their practices. Using an integrated marketing approach, our team helps law firms ensure that they are portraying a cohesive message to attract clients both online and offline.

We built our company on consulting with attorneys and providing them with guidance on establishing a proper web presence. One of our founders, Jabez LeBret, previously worked at Nordstrom. He brought with him the belief that you provide service to everyone, whether or not they are your customers. Our goal, above and beyond anything else, is to make sure that law firms have the right information before they make a decision. Sometimes that right decision is us, and sometimes it is not. If your firm is not the right fit for us, we would love the opportunity to send you to a trusted resource where we know you will be in good hands.

We have received many calls from attorneys who have read our book, and we are always happy to clear up any confusion regarding how to apply the information in this book to your web presence. If your firm has questions, we would be glad to answer them.

If you feel that your firm is one that we can help and you would like to find out about our team's availability to help you, please contact us:

Phone: (513) 444-2016

Email: jabez@gngf.com or mark@gngf.com

Web: http://www.GNGF.com

OUR CLE PROGRAMS: HOW TO BRING THE AUTHORS TO YOUR NEXT EVENT

State Bar
of NEW MEXICO

Jan. 10, 2014

Jabez LeBret
Get Noticed Get Found Inc.
1776 Mentor Ave #179
Cincinnati, OH 45212

Dear Jabez,

Thank you so much for speaking at the State Bar of New Mexico's 2013 CLE and Sand Nov. 25-27 in Costa Rica. As the keynote speaker who kicked off the event, you certainly captured our members' attention! The information, tips and advice you provided combined with your engaging presentation style earned much praise from attendees. After class hours in the hotel lobby, I saw you sitting with several members of our group who were very intent on continuing the discussion.

I am very appreciative of your ability to tailor the presentation to comply with our strict MCLE rules regarding law practice management courses. The topic of marketing does not qualify for credit; however, you were able to relate the creation of websites, use of social media and the importance of online presence to rules of ethics so MCLE would approve. You were well-prepared and knowledgeable of New Mexico rules.

In addition to your presentation at this event, I'd like to thank you and note a couple of times when you went above and beyond what I would expect of a presenter speaker. Not long after you arrived in the conference room and began setting up your own presentation, one of our members who would be making a presentation the next day asked for your assistance to show him how to make his photo presentation work with Windows 8. Although we were down to the wire with your presentation start time, you were not fazed. You helped him until he felt comfortable that he could run the presentation himself.

You continued helping with the program after your presentation. A retired New Mexico Supreme Court Justice spoke after you and upon arrival, he requested a podium. While I ran down the hall trying to find a hotel employee who could understand my hand signals of explaining what I needed (since I don't speak Spanish), you kept everything flowing in the conference room and even changed the set by moving the screen out of the way.

Jabez, I highly recommend you to any organization that is considering engaging you as a speaker. Please feel free to share this letter.

Sincerely,
Christine Morganti
Chief Operating Officer
New Mexico State Bar Association
5121 Masthead NE · P O Box 92860
Albuquerque, NM 87199-2860
(505) 797-6000 · (800) 876-6227
Fax (505) 828-3765 · www.nmbar.org

COLORADO BAR ASSOCIATION CLE

1900 Grant Street, Suite 300 • Denver, Colorado 80203-4303
Phone: (303) 860-0608 • Toll Free: (888) 860-2531 • Fax: (303) 860-0624
Web Site: www.cobar.org/cle • E-Mail: cle@cobar.org

In Colorado, Inc.   *The nonprofit educational arm of the Colorado Bar Association and the Denver Bar Association*

Dear Jabez,

Thanks so much for your recent presentation at our CLE Conference in Vail to nearly 350 attendees. Our goal was to have a plenary session that would appeal to many different types of lawyers who practice in a variety of substantive areas. Your presentation was just what we needed and the feedback, both in person and on our evaluations, was uniformly very positive. You engaged the audience within the first 2 minutes and held their attention for the entire presentation. I could tell by the crowd surrounding you that you generated a lot of interest from many who were in the audience who wanted to ask follow up questions and learn more about their online presence and the ethical guidelines for lawyers. Thanks again for a job well done and we hope to see you back here in Colorado.

With kind regards,

Gary Abrams, Executive Director

How To Bring The Authors To Your Next Event or CLE:

For a certain number of CLE's we will waive our speaking fee and travel expenses as part of our book tour. To find out if your bar association fits our book tour schedule please contact us directly at:

GNGF
CLE Program
513.444.2016
or email CLE@gngf.com

Both Mark Homer and Jabez LeBret have delivered more than 1,200 presentations combined. Since the first edition of this book, GNGF has delivered more than 75 CLEs, keynoted at several state bar annual events, and presented at legal industry and digital marketing events around the country.

We currently offer many different CLEs, and in most states, these CLEs qualify for up to 3.0 credits and can include an optional ethics credit. For a full list of courses, please visit https://gngf.com/cle-speaking/.

Our CLE Programs for Bar Associations and Legal Events

"The attendance was excellent, and I was amazed to see the high quality of evaluations returned. Almost everyone gave both of you, the speakers, and the topic a 5 out of a possible 5 score."

Peter Steiner,
Executive Director, Sonoma County Bar Association

Social Media Competence

This is not about how to use social media; rather, this course outlines how to properly advise your clients about the risks and liabilities when they use social media networks. We will also discuss using social media as evidence and understanding judicial holds. The recent comment to ABA Model Rule 1.1: Competence includes technology. We predict that it won't be long before lawyers are required to understand the basics of how social media functions. In reality, if you want to effectively advise your clients on the impact of their behavior, you need to have a clear understanding of how social media platforms work. If you are going to trial, you may need to be able to communicate about various social platforms.

What Attorneys Will Learn:

Focus Area #1: How People Use Social Media
in Their Daily Lives

Focus Area #2: Facebook, Twitter, Instagram,
Pinterest, and More

Focus Area #3: Judicial Holds and Deleting
Social Media Information

Focus Area #4: Discovering Issues Around Social Media

Focus Area #5: When Is Something Public and
When Is It Private?

After this course, you will be able to guide your clients more effectively, communicate clearly regarding issues surrounding publishing on social networks, and know which possible areas should be avoided for ethical reasons. From the client to the court room, this course covers it all.

The Ethics of Marketing for Lawyers

The year 2015 is here, and many things have changed with concerns to your online presence. We will walk you through the ethics of establishing a successful online marketing presence and show you how to utilize Avvo, Google, social media, and other tools that can boost your firm's online prowess.

What Attorneys Will Learn:

Focus Area #1: Ethically and Properly Establishing Your Website

Focus Area #2: Ethical Issues Surrounding
Reviews and Solicitation

Focus Area #3: Online Directory Listings and the
Ethics of Claiming a Listing

Focus Area #4: Content and Comparative Speech

Focus Area #5: Ethical Issues Surrounding
Posting on Social Media

Focus Area #6: Blogging: What You Can and Can't Do, Including
Client Confidentiality & Disclaimer Violations

This CLE delivers real, educational content that law firms need to navigate their online presence ethically. Once the CLE is complete, you will understand the best practices for ethically using the Internet, as well as how to avoid the traps of self-reviewing, improperly commenting on blogs, and misrepresenting your services online.

Practice Management

The practice management CLE ranges from one to three hours. It is also tailored to your state ethics and qualifies for ethics and general credit. There is an optional one-hour ethics portion for this CLE if you choose the three-hour option (two hours of practice management credit and one hour of ethics in total). We will cover the following focus areas as well as how specific programs, such as Clio or My Case, can help you in these areas.

What Attorneys Will Learn:

Focus Area #1: Tools for Time Management, Case
Management, and eSigning

Focus Area #2: Moving to the Cloud: Ethics and Tips

Focus Area #3: From Start to Finish: Intake Process,
Client Confidentiality, Follow-up

Focus Area #4: Going Paperless Does Not Mean No Paper

Following this CLE course, lawyers will understand the various technologies available to them to help improve how they deliver legal services, from time and billing to making filing dates and everything in between. We will walk through various hardware and software options available to the legal community. With all these types of activities, there is also a need to address the ethical implications and responsibilities for using such tools to provide legal services.

"As you can see from the enclosed evaluations, the attendees thoroughly enjoyed your presentation. One of the attendees said, "These guys are great, every attorney should attend this." Another attorney said, "They really know their stuff. I could have sat through an entire day learning and listening from them." Again, thank you for everything you did to ensure a successful seminar."

Jeannie Motylewski,
Executive Director, Lorain County Bar Association

ABOUT THE AUTHORS

Mark Homer

As co-founder and CEO of the law firm marketing agency GNGF, Mark uses a strong blend of technology, marketing, consulting, and management experience gained from his twenty years in the business world to lead the GNGF team in delivering targeted and efficient results with high-touch service. Mark gained in-depth business technology expertise at IBM, where his team helped develop some of the first corporate websites. As a co-founder of the marketing technology leader eshots, inc., he developed award-winning campaigns for many Fortune 500 brands. He gained experience in the legal industry during his years in Product Marketing for iManage (now HP Autonomy).

Mark has delivered presentations across the U.S. and internationally to business owners of all kinds, from attorneys to executives at Fortune 500 companies. When not managing the day-to-day operations at GNGF, Mark can usually be found coaching lacrosse or trying to brew up another batch of craft beer.

Follow Mark (@mark_homer) on Twitter.

Jabez LeBret

Jabez is co-author of the best-selling legal technology book Online Law Practice Strategies. He is the sitting co-chair of the Legal Marketing Association's (LMA) annual Your Honor Awards for excellence in legal marketing. Jabez was recently commissioned by the LMA to produce the Standardized Guide for legal marketing due in late 2015. He is an international technology expert who has delivered CLE presentations in over 30 states at bar associations, legal events, and annual conferences. Jabez writes a regular business and technology column for Forbes and is also a contributor to the ABA Journal, Clio, Avvo, and NBC Chicago. He is also co-founder of the legal marketing agency GNGF, winner of the 2014 Best Place to Work by the Cincinnati Business Courier and runner-up for Business of the Year by the Cincinnati Chamber of Commerce. Jabez sits on the SMB CAB advisory board for Box.com and is also on the San Francisco Entrepreneurs Organization's board. Over the last two years, Jabez has worked with SUBWAY on projects ranging from communications to managing GenY employees. He loves coffee and is a craft beer enthusiast."

Follow Jabez (@jabezlebret) on Twitter.